TEENAGERS, BE THE BEST YOU CAN BE

RECOMMENDED FOR PEOPLE OF ALL AGES

Kay Mielenz

Published by Divine Resources Inc.
with support from Old Mate Media, Sydney, AU

Manufactured in Littleton, Colorado, USA

First Edition

Imprint: Divine Resources For All

ISBN: 978-1-955713-08-5 (paperback)

ISBN: 978-1-955713-09-2 (eBook)

Library of Congress Control Number: 2021925240

CONTENTS

ABOUT THE AUTHOR

Kay Mielenz enjoyed careers in computer programming, real estate sales, and financial consulting. Now, as a grandmother, she directs her attention to today's teenagers who will be the leaders of tomorrow. They will have the responsibility to create fairness and respect for all people.

Kay's other works include *God Talks to All of Us,* a direct communication from divinity for all of humanity. In this book, God utilized Kay's ability to receive interdimensional communication to educate us in His own words. God explains why you are alive on Earth and leads you to recognize the importance of every person, without exception. He teaches that which is difficult to discern for oneself. This book empowers you to work towards the betterment of yourself, your children, and planet Earth.

God Talks to All of Us, Thoughts to Keep in Mind is a pocket-sized companion to *God Talks to All of Us.* This smaller book shines a spotlight on beneficial traits and qualities to expand within ourselves. *Thoughts to Keep in Mind* provides readers an easy way to reconnect with God's presence on a daily basis.

Kay has also authored, *What It Is Like to Die and What Comes After.* In this book, Kay documents the after-physical life goings-on, both positive and negative, utilizing her recorded conversations with deceased people. If you need proof of an afterlife, this book will deliver it to you in spades.

After writing these three books, it was clear to Kay that she needed to address the challenges that teenagers face every day. *Teenagers, Be the Best You Can Be* applies to adults as well as teenagers. This book shows all people how to strive for excellence in their attitudes, perceptions, and behaviors and points out how to be a very successful person.

ABOUT THE BOOK

Teenage years are filled with excitement, awkward feelings of insecurity, and vast potential to achieve. Few teenagers comprehend their importance. The teenagers of today are the leaders of tomorrow. *Teenagers, Be the Best You Can Be* supports all people to strive to be the best person they can be. Every individual will be inspired to view themself more supportively as they proceed through this book.

Achievement is about performance, how a person thinks and behaves. Everyone has vast potential to excel in three ways. The first way is in their perception of what creates an outstanding individual. The answer to this does not include dollars and cents. The second way is by removing needless obstacles to accepting all people as precious and worthy of respect. The third way is in honoring oneself, as well as every other person.

Teenagers, Be the Best You Can Be helps teenagers build confidence and create a successful and satisfying life, one that honors their individuality and spirit. This book is a handbook of enlightenment for every teenager and adult who wants to be the best person they can be and contribute to the betterment of humanity and our planet Earth. We all need to pull together to advance perceptions and behaviors. Doing this will give us greater life satisfaction and build a better tomorrow for all.

INTRODUCTION

Teenagers are powerhouses in the making. Today's teenagers will carry society forward with innovations and improvements in commerce, medicine, and science. All teenagers are needed to advance society and support those who tend to be left behind.

Today's teenagers have the capacity to right the wrongs of the past, particularly in the areas of race relations and other forms of prejudice, the protection of our environment, and expressing compassion to all others. Our world needs teenagers to stand up for minorities and the disadvantaged, showing older generations what they should have been doing all along.

Entering one's teenage years indicates that it is time for a great leap forward in one's understanding of their capability to impact society. Obviously, older generations have not been successful in equalizing the playing field for minorities, recognizing the importance of every person, or protecting our environment. Teenagers, do not hold back from always striving to do your best to excel in your school work and in developing and affirming a strong moral code of conduct.

CHAPTER ONE
YOU ARE IMPORTANT

—

Heads up, teenagers. Take the reins of leadership and become your planet Earth's best friends. Under your watch, Earth will prosper or fail. There is much that each of you can do to put protective arms around your planet, but you must act immediately. You are a powerful force, which can steer the direction that humanity takes. Unite with other like-minded teenagers who care deeply about the well-being of your planetary home and get to work.

Focus on your talents, characteristics, and capabilities. Do not discount your positive attributes by comparing yourself with anyone else. Each person is unique. One may have similar talents and abilities as other people, but each person's uniqueness displays itself in their expression of these capabilities.

There are glamorous talents and skills and others that do not have a bright light shining on them. Some people crave the spotlight, and others are not comfortable displaying their aptitudes in front of others. There is space for everyone to fit in and be comfortable.

All teenagers are potential powerhouses of innovative ideas and contributions. These powerhouses tend to look in a mirror and fail to see the vast and wondrous potential they possess. More often than not, teenagers discount themselves while glamorizing others. Their self-esteem becomes wobbly when they do that.

I suggest that every teenager think of themself as a very worthwhile person, who does not have to draw attention to themself in any way. Some of the showboats are just displaying their true nature. Others may feel insecure and are showing off to build their self-esteem. Regardless of the reason, each person needs to accept that their natural self-expression is good enough.

Every person is worthwhile. During teenage years, self-assessments bounce all over the place. Those who do not fit in with the glamorous groups feel left out.

Few teenagers go through their teen years with permanent self-esteem. Usually, their self-esteem bobs up and down. Anything from being ignored by uppity others to not having a friend to sit with during lunchtime pulls teenagers down.

Transferring to a new school when the student does not know any of the other students is one of the most difficult situations, especially for a teenager who tends to be introverted. Those who are naturally extroverted have a big advantage when they are in unfamiliar surroundings. They relish announcing their arrival and have a knack for drawing people to them.

The human race is diverse. **Each person is unique, and each has unlimited potential to contribute to the good of all.** At this time, I am appealing to all teenagers everywhere to come together to rescue planet Earth from continuing to be subjected to humanity's neglect. You are the leaders of tomorrow, and I am counting on you to save your planet from its spiraling decline.

Older generations have sidestepped responsibility for safeguarding Earth for the generations to come. You know what that means. You are next at-bat, and you need to hit a home run.

You are young and energized, and you know right from wrong. Do not wait for your elders to suddenly become responsible citizens of planet Earth. They have already demonstrated their disinterest in going out of their way to undertake planetary responsibility. Your generation has the most to lose by ignoring the dire consequences that lie ahead.

Each of you is of primary importance. Each of you is a powerhouse of ingenuity, creativity, and productivity. That which you produce will form civilized society throughout this century. Do not settle for what you see around you now. Go beyond current attitudes and behaviors to forge a new path.

Turn your attention to the kindness factor. This factor is missing in many people's lives. I will describe the kindness factor as I see it. First, be kind to yourself. **Do not criticize yourself for any reason. Instead, accept what you perceive as your shortcomings as potential areas for you to improve.** Know that you and everyone else are precious and equal in importance to each other, regardless of any imperfections you may notice within yourself. Every person is precious, and this includes every one of you.

Finding faults within other people and then focusing on them does not improve one's character. Give yourself no reason to ignore, ridicule, or insult another person. Instead, give yourself every reason to take note of your shortcomings and make a plan to evolve yourself out of continuing to cling to them. Refresh your self-expression and display yourself as equal to all others and superior to none.

Include in your life kindness to all people, viewing every person as special in their own way. Look beyond the pizzazz factor and do not only be impressed by those of high achievement. Look for good, solid decency, and a sensitive, kind heart in those you draw to yourself. Create a welcoming world where people can count on one another to be gracious, accepting, and supportive.

The world will not change to become a more supportive and humane place to live unless teenagers outshine the older generations with sensitivity and kindness, beyond that which is typical in your world today. I advise all teenagers to take the lead in displaying the traits and qualities that humanity needs to express to evolve to the point of being kind, compassionate, and benevolent. Every person has inherent goodness at the core of his or her being. Sometimes this quality does not show. As individuals lead their lives, their goodness remains covered because their point of focus remains on their worries, fears, and desires.

If you could wash yourself clean of your worries and fears when you bathe, your lives would be easier to manage. As it is, there is no soap known to dissolve unmanageable human tendencies. However, there is free will and determination, which powers individuals to achieve beyond their expectations.

I advise teenagers to empower themselves with a clear vision of their importance in shaping the world of tomorrow. You are the ones who can turn society in a healthier direction than what you see around you now. You have a clearer vision than your predecessors have had, and you have more at risk. You will face the brunt of making some tough decisions to maintain planet Earth's viability for the generations to come. Unfortunately, many older folks dismiss the need for safeguarding planet Earth, using the lame excuse that they will no longer be alive when conditions upon our planet become disastrous because of humanity's recklessness.

Now is the time to commit to your planetary home's well-being. She is dependent upon you and your generation. Thus far, there has been insufficient attention paid to her well-being, and no generation has taken it upon themselves to champion her sustainability.

In the years ahead, the lazy ones who do nothing to support your planet's viability will regret their shortsightedness. Mother Earth has the right to protect herself. The disrespect shown to her may come back to roost on all humanity.

Your beloved planet Earth needs champions to safeguard her. She is dependent upon those she serves to take care of her. No one can say that your planetary home is not essential. All people are dependent upon her generosity to feed, clothe and shelter them.

Who among you is ready and willing to become planet Earth's champion? Who is willing to stand up for your precious planet? Step forward, teenagers. **Lead the rest of humanity to come to their senses and recognize the importance of protecting Earth's well-being.**

Older populations have been lax in their responsibility to safeguard their planet, as is obvious by the pollution on land and sea, which threatens the purity of the food supply. Big businesses, bent on increasing their profitability by reducing the purity of their products, have abandoned their predecessors' former high-quality production standards. The older generations looked the other way as the big food production corporations lowered standards that had been in place to protect the quality of the food supply.

Have you heard the adage, "You are what you eat"? Do you know what you are eating? Unless your family purchases only organic food, you are eating chemical additives businesses have added to the food you eat. People do not thrive on chemical additives. Only the pocketbooks of the large corporations, which produce the chemical additives, thrive.

Teenagers, pull together and accomplish what your elders failed to accomplish. Take a firm stand for purity within the food supply and reap the benefits that this would bring to everyone's physical body. Champion the cause of wholesome food and pure water to benefit all people.

Some nations are wiser than others are. Those nations reject putrefying their food supply with chemicals. They are more caring about their populations' health and well-being.

Some people are wiser than others are. Some corporations are more ethical than others are. Ethical corporations do not market products that debilitate physical bodies in order to increase their profitability.

Greed drives some corporations to take unethical steps to make more money. Some companies sell highly profitable products without concern for the health and well-being of their patrons. The profits made by greed-driven corporations create a stain on the company when they sell products that are detrimental to their uninformed consumer's well-being.

Teenagers, it is time for you to become more aware of what goes on in the world around you. You cannot afford to trust that older generations are making sound decisions. Do not place your well-being in the hands of negligent lawmakers who do not support high standards for your food supply.

Step forward as a group to insist that genetically modified food be taken off the shelves of markets and discarded as not being fit for human or animal consumption. You need to take responsibility for the purity of your food supply. Your older generations behaved like meek lambs when the primary producer of genetically modified seeds sold those, who had responsibility for approval of this new idea, a bill of goods.

Teenagers, it is up to you to become more aware of the importance of what you put into your bodies. Begin with avoiding genetically modified foods whenever you can, and then progress to consuming the purest and least tampered with food. Grow your own gardens in the summer months for the healthy food they will produce and the pure joy of tasting the nutritious gifts Mother Nature provides in your own backyard.

Teenagers, you are the guardians of tomorrow. You may not feel that you are especially important right now, but you have a tremendous responsibility in front of you. As you form the world of tomorrow, your challenge is to improve upon past practices, which are irrational, non-productive, or unfair.

You have good moral fiber within you and a natural sense of the growing power within you. You are moving from a state of dependence into a full-blown leadership position within your families and potentially within your societies. I urge you to determine to act for the good of all. Pull together and create a fair world for all people.

Teenagers, you have more power than you might suspect. When you pull together for a common cause, you can get things done. Make your voices heard, and you will draw support from many in the older generations, who need your generation to enlighten them and lead them to stand up for what is right for all of humanity.

Each of you is of primary importance.

Each of you is a powerhouse of ingenuity, creativity, and productivity.

Teenagers, you are the guardians of tomorrow.

CHAPTER TWO

ASSUME A LEADERSHIP POSITION

——

Teenagers, set an example for the older generations to follow. You are capable of mobilizing your combined efforts to awaken the rest of society to the urgent situation at hand. You have more at risk than your elders, and you have more potential to think independently.

Do not be led astray by mindlessly following past traditions when the world needs fresh new approaches. It is your turn. You are up to bat. Your generation comes next as the decider of how the future will look and what it will be like for you and your contemporaries.

I am concerned that you, as a group, are unaware of your vast potential to assume a leadership position among those who are older and supposedly wiser. Do not assume that you are on the low end of the totem pole because of your age. You may be less experienced than older generations, but consider that you are also less encumbered by marching in lockstep with established ways.

You can be your own deciders. You can think independently and forge a better path for yourselves and for the rest of the world to follow. Do not believe that you are less important than adults are. You have something valuable that they do not have.

You have fresh attitudes and ideas. Older generations tend to adapt and keep going. Most of them have settled for following their leader, sometimes thoughtlessly. They are more likely to buy into *the way things are,* ignoring how much better things could be.

Teenagers, assume your rightful position alongside your elders. It is time for you to become involved in creating much-needed modifications in general attitudes and behaviors. You can make yourselves a force for the common good instead of surrendering your power to the older generations.

Use your minds and your hearts. Determine what is rational and compassionate. Do not sit back and think that you are powerless until you reach the age of twenty-one.

First, you must engage your awareness. Look around and take an inventory of what you think is good and productive within society. Then consider what you would like to see improved. Now I am not referring to the small matters. I am looking for issues that are significant to many people.

There are fundamental areas of importance, such as how people value other people. Valuing and respecting all others is at the top of the list for wise and compassionate people. Powerful people who have a strong can-do attitude may form an entire list of contributions they are interested in making to support those in need. Entertainers may think of ways to bring their specialties to those who enjoy what they have to offer. There are many ways to reach out to needy others with various kinds of support.

If you spend your days without noticing how you can make a contribution of some sort to another person, you are not taking full advantage of the innate goodness within yourself. **The best thing you can do for your self-esteem is to step up to defend or assist another person. Think fairness.**

Do whatever you can to make the playing field fair for everyone. Extend a hand to the less fortunate to boost them up. Share your excess with others who may be having a hard time getting by. Life does not treat everyone evenly, but kindhearted individuals can help level the playing field for others.

I encourage all teenagers to demonstrate the goodness within them by extending themselves to aid others. When one feels good about themself, they are more likely to be interested in helping others. When people think poorly about themselves, they may not have the internal strength to consider how they could assist another.

Life's difficulties drag a person down. Be sure you do not over dwell on what is wrong. If you do, you will make it more difficult to pull yourself up into smooth waters once again.

Being a teenager is challenging but also freeing. The teenage years are empowering, as teenagers take the helm of deciding where their interests and talents lay. No one is suited for everything. Each person has the adventure of discovering what their particular interests are.

Most high schools have extracurricular offerings such as sports, debate, music, theatre, and newspaper and yearbook production. There are many ways for teenagers to explore their hidden talents by following their interests. It is exhilarating to pursue your interests and discover that you have an aptitude in that area.

Teenagers, go forward with enthusiasm to explore the wondrous talents and capabilities that each of you possess. Be adventuresome and attempt the activities that attract you. Go forward and do not hold back because of insecurities. Most teenagers have heightened insecurities, so you are not the only one if this is your experience. The challenge for most teenagers is to overcome their self-doubt.

Self-doubt is especially common in teenagers. Many parents do not do enough to encourage and support their teenagers.

Some parents set high goals for their children that turn out to be unreasonable. Teenagers, I have some important advice for you. Navigate your own ship into healthy waters.

Search within yourself for the instinct to go in one direction or another. You have a guiding compass within yourself. Certainly, pay attention to what a parent or a respected other person suggests, but reserve the decision for yourself. Follow your interests and your instincts. If they are wholesome, you will be on the right path.

Teenage years are exploration years. I suggest that teenagers explore themselves to find the beauty and uniqueness within them. **Teenagers are God's gifts to tomorrow for all of humanity.** They are going to perform the heavy lifting for humanity in the decades ahead. Their participation and leadership will be essential to the rest of the population in the future.

Placed within every person are aptitudes and abilities, so do not presume that you are not as important as others are. Every person has contributions to make. Your world needs all of you to step up and participate in making your world a better place. Do not hang back and think that you do not have anything significant to contribute.

It may take a while to figure out where your strengths are. So, I urge you to investigate all areas that draw your interest before settling on your path. Sometimes combining two or more interests brings sharply focused, very satisfying opportunities to utilize more of your innate capabilities.

Teenagers, hold no prejudice against yourself. Respect yourself and do not denigrate yourself. Embrace solid, good conduct, and you will shine without trying to draw attention to yourself. Be comfortable in your own shoes, and do not wish that your shoes were different. Each person has uniqueness, which deserves to be honored.

Do not hold back from appreciating yourself. Recognize your good traits and qualities. How will you know what to emphasize if you do not slow down enough to analyze yourself? How will you address your weaker areas, building strengths from weaknesses, if you do not even think of such matters? Do not bumble your way through life when you can take charge and create the best path for yourself going forward.

Think long-range. Do not become upset with minor difficulties or disappointments. Teenagers tend to blow up minor challenges instead of taking them in stride. As one gains strength and resilience by tackling life's problems, one gains emotional and psychological stability. These are the building blocks of responsible adulthood.

Teenagers are like a flower that is about to bloom. The flower is about to emerge from a bud that appears to be like all the other buds. However, each flower, when it blooms, will be like none other. Each flower is a masterpiece on its own, to be admired and enjoyed. **Consider yourself an emerging powerhouse that can confront any obstacle and overcome it as you mature into adulthood.**

Do not be hesitant to make errors as you mature. Errors are part of forging ahead with life. Not every choice or decision that you make will pay dividends, but always do your best and know that success can, at times, come from apparent failure. Examples of success stemming from failure are the multitudes of inventions that failed to perform the function the inventor envisioned but worked aptly to perform an alternative purpose.

If you do not put your best foot forward and take action, you will never know the full extent of what you have within yourself. Each teenager is bubbling over with potential to contribute to the common good. Taken as a group, teenagers are capable of holding adults to higher standards. When teenagers step forward as a group to demand fair and ethical treatment of every person, they will teach their elders and demonstrate fundamental humanitarian concerns that ought to be on everyone's plate.

I encourage teenagers to take off their insecurities and their self-doubt. Do not hold on to them as if they were family treasures. They are liabilities that do not need to be present.

Do away with attitudes and beliefs that undermine a can-do conviction. **Know yourselves as powerhouses of potential to change the world for the better. Identify what you can do to make your world fair and supportive to all of humanity.**

Push forward with a mindset to act with fairness to all. Push forward, honoring and respecting all others, as well as yourself. Push forward, creating a more wholesome and supportive world for all people. Use yourselves as role models for the rest.

Give yourselves the satisfaction that you are standing up for what is right and good for all people. Your elders failed to take responsibility for the well-being of all people. It is time for the younger generations to accomplish that which the older generations failed to perform.

Search within yourself for the instinct to go in one direction or another. You have a guiding compass within yourself.

Know yourselves as powerhouses of potential to change the world for the better. Identify what you can do to make your world fair and supportive to all of humanity.

Give yourselves the satisfaction that you are standing up for what is right and good for all people.

CHAPTER THREE

ACKNOWLEDGE YOUR IMPORTANCE

—

What makes a successful life? If you ask three different people for their opinion, you may receive three different answers. Would you like to know a good way to define a successful life? When a person gains honorable satisfaction by producing something of value for others, whether it be food, entertainment, or heart surgery, and, if along the way, they treasure every person with whom they interact, they are living a meaningful life.

Every person has the capacity to lead a meaningful life. Teenagers owe it to themselves to follow their inner inclinations and investigate their interests. Be honest with yourself. Do not select an area of interest mainly because the rewards are outstanding. One does not sign up for the paycheck. One signs up for the satisfaction of having the opportunity to follow their interests and express their unique talents.

See yourselves as precious gems. Each of you has preciousness within you. Each of you has goodness with you. However, many of you hide your true self from view because you do not feel that you measure up to the prima donnas who quickly latch on to the spotlight. Precious gems do not need spotlights to reveal their beauty.

One trait, in particular, is most refreshing. People who are satisfied being themselves, as they are, and shy away from puffing themselves up to seek attention, are a delight. This type of behavior is a wholesome way to be, an honest way to live.

Some people are outgoing and attention-seeking as their natural way to be. They are successful at gaining the attention that they savor. Their challenges are in sharing the spotlight and going beyond ego gratification. Introverted people are less likely to crave the spotlight; however, everyone enjoys acknowledgment for their accomplishments.

The way teenagers look at things has a lot to do with their family's impact upon them. When a teenager is on the receiving end of harsh treatment from one of their family members, their lights do not shine as brightly as they would if they had received consistent warmth and respectful treatment. One's self-esteem is partly a product of the respect shown to them by other people. It is hard to hold one's head up with confidence when being looked down upon by others.

I encourage teenagers to develop sound self-concepts. Recognize all of your positive qualities. Keep these as the cornerstone of who you are. Look for these traits in particular: putting forth your best effort and extending kindness to all. Also, include a willingness to assist those who could use a helping hand. These types of qualities form the basis of high integrity.

Maintaining a strong standard of integrity builds self-esteem and high self-concepts. If you want to feel good about yourself, act beneficially towards other people. Doing this will make you feel good inside.

The more you factor in what is in other people's best interests and determine to act as a force for good, the more your self-esteem will flourish. Do not forget about your own best interests; just be sure to pay attention to the best interests of others as well. **Everyone seeking the best for others, as well as themselves, creates a better world.**

Teenagers, your world mainly revolves around your schooling, your home life, and hopefully, your responsibilities. Embrace your responsibilities. Becoming a responsible, dependable person builds self-confidence, which will carry you far for the rest of your life. Even in your younger years, you are preparing to lead a meaningful, responsible life. Nearly everyone who applies themself discovers that they have more capability than they thought they had.

Teenagers, recognize your potential to alter society, making it more fair and equitable for all people. You, as a group, share the responsibility of your generation to build more support for each other and the rest of humanity. You can provide more support than the world has seen in the past or as it typically sees now. Your generation has a heavy load to carry, and you need to depend on each other as equal partners.

Look at what you are inheriting; problems, inequality, and insufficiency for many people. Many people have nowhere to turn for a helping hand. Others, who could be stepping up to assist, look the other way, as if those needing assistance were not important. For the most part, your elders have ignored the plight of those who struggle to get by, inwardly thankful that they are not among them.

I am calling on all teenagers to imagine themselves in the shoes of those who are disadvantaged. Ask yourself how you would feel about going to school hungry, dressed in ragged hand-me-downs or ill-fitting clothes from a charity. How would you build your self-esteem if your hand-me-down shoes were two sizes too large for your feet?

Typically, the teenage years are a time of self-absorption and insecurity. The insecurity increases every time a teenager is in an uncomfortable situation. Parental faultfinding often is to blame when teenagers pull back from being self-assured and confident. Rarely do parents recognize how tender-hearted and vulnerable teenagers often are. Feuding parents, without realizing what they are doing, often cause their children to lose emotional stability.

Teenagers, be your own "port in the storm". When someone creates a storm of conflict, let it be his or hers, but not yours. Keep yourself directed on the right path without wavering, riding above the storm instead of allowing yourself to become swallowed up in it. There is a lot to be said for becoming unflappable.

An unflappable person prefers to ride a smooth current rather than a tumultuous current. Riding a smooth current provides opportunities to think rationally in order to gain a clearer understanding of others' perspectives. When one becomes over-enamored with their perception, without considering other's viewpoints, the best decisions are not forthcoming.

It is one thing to contribute and another to dominate. A person who insists on having his or her way, which is obviously irrational, is attempting to dominate. Do not follow the leader if the leader is more interested in flexing their muscles than providing reasonable potential solutions. Wanting to be the person in charge will not produce the most desirable leadership when one is mainly after ego gratification.

Do not be over-impressed by those with flash and dash. Attention-seeking people catch others' attention, which they find very satisfying. However, being the center of attention is not for everyone. Do not overlook the quiet, reflective people who are not comfortable in the spotlight. These are often deep thinkers who may be miles ahead of the rest when it comes to problem-solving.

Teenage years are years of discovery. It is as if the world is broadening, expanding, and opening in new ways for you to enjoy. Schoolwork is becoming more complex. Learning seems to leap forward instead of chugging along. Year by year, teenagers expand their perceptions as their school subjects open new worlds to them.

These years provide teenagers an opportunity to begin to acknowledge their importance. In the years to come, teenagers will become earnest contributors to the general population. The rest of the age groups will look to this new generation to improve the older generations' standards and accomplishments. It is one thing to follow in the footsteps of wise elders. In addition, it is even more important to integrate improvements into the way things have been.

Teenagers, value yourselves as a crucially important segment of society. Take this time, your teenage years, to prepare yourselves to carry the responsibility that will be yours in the future. Know how important you are to the generations to come, and consider how you would like to see our world and our societies develop more respect and support for all people. Yours is the generation to push forward moral, ethical behavior, which far surpasses that which is currently displayed.

Yours is the generation to place supportive, caring arms around all people. You will demonstrate your humanity by standing up for those who need support that you can give. See the preciousness within every individual and celebrate the beauty within human beings. Create a world of kindness, friendship, and honoring of every individual.

You are in a unique position. **You are important because of what you can accomplish that past generations have not.** You can unify and uplift because you have observed other people's suffering. You know how to reach out to others with kindness and concern for their well-being. You want the world to be a friendlier, safer place for everyone, and you want to be part of making it so.

You represent the future for a more fair and equitable world in which to live. Each of you has an important part to play. Every time you extend yourself, being respectful and helpful to another person, you exercise your preciousness. Every time you support another person with a kind word or a helping hand, you honor that person's humanity. When you honor another person's humanity, you honor your own as well.

The more you factor in what is in other people's best interests and determine to act as a force for good, the more your self-esteem will flourish.

Teenagers,
be your own "port in the storm".
When someone creates a storm of conflict, let it be his or hers, but not yours.

You represent the future for a more fair and equitable world in which to live. Each of you has an important part to play.

CHAPTER FOUR

YOU HAVE TREMENDOUS POTENTIAL

—

Every person has their own life to live. Some people's life situations are obviously more challenging than other people's circumstances. However, everyone's life includes both hardships and delights.

Brace yourself, teenagers. No longer are you going to be coddled. It is time to step up to the plate and prove to yourself that you have unlimited potential within yourself.

Do not be afraid to tackle new endeavors. It is time to expand your concept of what is possible for you to accomplish. Do not be a dreamer who fantasizes about doing things without actually stepping forward to accomplish their aspirations. Get up your courage. Take a determined step in the direction of your longing.

You have tremendous potential, so do not hold yourself back from utilizing every bit of it. Many teenagers underrate themselves. Have you heard the term *nothing ventured, nothing gained*? Do not hold yourself back. Press forward with determination to bring out the best in yourself.

You have nothing to lose by attempting something new. You will not know if you have the capability to succeed unless you go in that direction. It is frustrating to look back and think about what could have been. Do not disappoint yourself. Follow your inclinations. Potentially, you will gain new skills and increased self-confidence.

Discard any predisposition to pull yourself back from becoming involved in activities that appeal to you. Investigate your interests. **Every person has aptitudes and capabilities that they may be unaware of having. Every person has unique ways of stretching in new directions, thereby expanding their individual fulfillment.**

Think outside the box. Some activities seem reserved for those who prepared themselves with experience. If you are interested in a particular activity but lack experience, try out anyway. You may attract the attention of the teacher or coach sponsoring the activity, who may accept you, even as a beginner.

Interest sparks a desire to achieve, which is appealing to educators. Utilize every opportunity that comes your way. Have confidence in yourself and your ability to learn. Summon your courage and step forward.

Every person has remarkable potential to achieve more than they anticipate. Do not predefine what you can or cannot accomplish unless you have a valid reason. Leave the door open to discovering more capabilities than you anticipated. Outperform your expectations.

Very few people utilize all their potential. Predetermined opinions regarding one's probable effectiveness may lead teenagers to avoid stretching themselves. Too many teenagers do not give themselves a chance to succeed because they inaccurately pass a negative judgment on their capability.

No one can know what he or she is capable of doing, or not capable of doing, until they test themself. Go forward with an open mind and your best effort to experience new activities. You may surprise and delight yourself by finding a good fit or unexpectedly identifying a related alternative. Teenagers, stretch your perception of what you can accomplish. Give your efforts a chance to speak for themselves.

Teenagers, your job is to put in your best effort throughout your teenage years and thereafter. Do not think you will be different as an adult than you are as a teenager. The same predispositions you develop as a teenager will remain with you when you reach adulthood.

If, as a teenager, you attend class regularly and on time, you display the traits of consistency, reliability, and maturity. When you complete your assignments on time, you demonstrate dependability. These traits are essential components of success in the workplace.

The way you go about living your life as a teenager predicts your success as an adult. When you hold yourself to high morals and ethics, you will develop self-esteem and be admired as a teenager and throughout your life. When you go out of your way to help another person, you demonstrate kindness, compassion, and humanitarianism. Developing these admirable qualities also builds one's self-esteem.

With high self-esteem, people feel more content with themselves. They tend to be happier and more self-satisfied. Happy people make the world a more pleasant place.

When people remain on the sunny side of life, they enhance their enjoyment and make a positive impact on other people. Sometimes all a person needs to uplift their spirits is for a friend or neighbor to smile and say hello. A simple gesture by one person often delights another.

When a person dwells on themself to the point of discounting the importance of other people, they are likely to live a shallow life. Life's richness arises from one's interactions with others. The simple act of smiling is inviting as it connotes warmth and happiness.

Grumpy people carry a dark cloud, which may envelop those with whom they interact. Their grumpiness originates within themselves, although such people typically attribute their poor temperament to whatever they can pin it on. The problem with grumpy people is that they usually pull other people down as well.

Everyone has up days and down days. One of life's challenges is to navigate difficult times without negatively affecting oneself or other people. Some people like to create drama for themselves and others. They stir up a little trouble and then walk away.

Dishing up problems to throw other people off balance is a poor way to express oneself. Forget theatrics and express yourself wholesomely. Keep your relationships on the solid ground of respecting all others.

Always give that which you prefer to receive. Only dish out what you would be satisfied receiving in return. Forget about elevating some people while looking down on others. Instead, treasure every person as a friend and interact with all people graciously.

Teenagers, you are about to determine what will happen to you in the years ahead. Give yourself every advantage. Practice the four steps to success for all teenagers.

Put yourself on all the right radar screens. Become known as a dependable student who takes their schoolwork seriously. Go out of your way to help others. Be gracious, kind, and inclusive to everyone.

The teenage years are a time of growing independence, so do not cling to room service at home. Make your presence appreciated by pitching in to take care of your own needs, such as doing your laundry and cleaning your room. You will feel good about shouldering these responsibilities as you recognize that you are building skills, as well as good character within yourself.

The best thing for you is to build self-confidence. With self-confidence, you will go forward unafraid of disappointing yourself. Avoid putting up roadblocks that come from bathing in self-doubt. Scrub any self-doubt out of yourself by setting yourself up for success.

No one can know what he or she is capable of doing, or not capable of doing, until they test themself. Go forward with an open mind and your best effort to experience new activities.

Teenagers,
stretch your perception of what you can accomplish.

CHAPTER FIVE
INSTITUTE CHANGE

Teenagers, I am giving you a little tip, something of which you may not be aware. Your importance is beyond your ability to perceive. **Each of you is a treasure and a blessing.**

Every person has goodness within them. Along the way, some people easily express their innate goodness while other people keep their goodness hidden, sometimes even from themselves. Never be afraid to let your inner goodness shine forth. Make choices and decisions from your base of inner goodness and enjoy the feelings of well-being that you will generate.

Teenagers, you may not realize how skilled you are becoming at problem-solving. Your lives are peppered with decisions to make and problems to solve. You are practicing this skill so that you can enter adulthood with confidence that you will successfully navigate your own boat.

Challenges are good for you, as long as they are appropriate. If you receive a life challenge that is overwhelming and you do not feel capable of navigating the challenge alone, do not hesitate to seek support from caring others who are compassionate and rational. Sometimes other perspectives open avenues that one did not perceive on their own. Feedback and advice from supportive others may spark one to expand their list of potential solutions until the best one becomes obvious.

I suggest that you look upon yourselves as future governors of how the world will be in the years and decades ahead.

Going forward, respect your intelligence and your importance. You are becoming educated, so you will be able to construct a more humane model for humanity to follow instead of blindly following how things have been in the past.

Openly accept the differences in people and respect those who come from different parts of the world. Look fondly on those from varying economic backgrounds and those who want to change the world for the betterment of humanity. Create more fluidity within society, doing away with the rigidity of continuing past ways which are deficient.

Teenagers, you represent hope for the future. Your challenge is no small undertaking. Your world is not a pleasant place to be for a great many people. Inequity abounds. Cruelty is common. Some people's arrogance steps on the well-being of those who are in tough situations. Who would be pleased to be born into a world where much of the population suffers from inequity and severe challenges?

Do not think of yourselves as unable to institute change for the better. You are the only ones who can create change for the better. The rest of society has adjusted to the way things are and demonstrate little interest in improving their current established behaviors. You have a clearer perception than many of your elders and more compassion. Step forward to become tomorrow's leaders.

If you pull together as a determined force to be reckoned with, you can imprint society with higher standards and more concern about the well-being of those who are less fortunate. You can join loving, caring others in an effort to uplift the well-being of everyone. I suggest that in helping others, one actually helps themselves. One of the reasons we are living on Earth is to test and improve ourselves.

Earth is a schoolhouse, and every person on Earth is a student. Even older adults learn life lessons simply by going through daily activities. Our lifetimes offer us the opportunity to become more honest, humane, and generous-spirited. Many people equate success in life to how much money they make, using financial gain as their barometer of success. Creating a high net worth is not as significant an achievement as being a genuinely honest and caring person.

The epitome of human advancement is within reach of every person, but most people are unaware of how to achieve this lofty goal. Many people keep their eye on dollars and cents. The more that is in their pocket, the more successful they determine themselves to be. Someone can steal another person's dollars and cents, but no one can steal another person's determination to live a life of respect and caring for all people.

Teenagers, do not hold yourselves back from striving to fulfill your dreams and aspirations and learn to trust your inner knowing. At times, one's inner knowing bypasses rationality, so do not be too strict with what you will allow yourself to consider. Be honest with yourself and examine your reasoning behind the important decisions you are making.

You may not yet be at the point of deciding which occupational path to take, but it is not too soon to begin to define which areas interest you. I have some advice. If you come close to fainting at the sight of blood, do not plan to become a surgeon.

If you enjoy cooking for other people, you may be interested in becoming a chef. Do not panic if you are without ideas about what you would like to have as your occupation. Identify your unique talents and interests and consider employment opportunities that utilize both aspects.

Do not pressure yourself to make a decision. Keep the door open to whatever possibilities come to mind. Anticipate an obvious choice while holding open the potential for an unexpected idea to come to the forefront of your considerations. Whatever you do, do not worry that you will not find your own unique direction. At the right time, your best choice will become apparent.

Teenagers, the world is yours to contribute to and yours to enjoy. You do not have to follow a path that does not suit you. If family members want you to follow a particular path that does not resonate within you, as something you are interested in, beware. You may not want to discount relatives' feelings or expectations, but you must captain your own boat.

Do not limit yourselves. Do not think, "I can't go to college because our family cannot afford it." Investigate avenues such as scholarships, loans, grants, and a part-time job to make it possible. Take the word *can't* out of your vocabulary. Determination pays off but only when you employ it.

Will power works. The combination of a strong will and determination can remove what appear to be insurmountable roadblocks. Determination is like gasoline in your car; it keeps you moving toward your destination.

Each of you is a treasure and a blessing.

Do not think of yourselves as unable to institute change for the better. You are the only ones who can create change for the better.

CHAPTER SIX

EMPHASIZE YOUR POSITIVE TRAITS

As teenagers mature, their self-esteem begins to solidify. Instead of being wobbly as it may have been in the past, their self-esteem firms and expands with broadening achievements. Success breeds success. There is nothing better for a teenager than rising up to a challenge and then conquering their fears and insecurities to reach higher and go further than they expected.

Every stage of development has bonuses attached. When a teenager conquers shyness, they enjoy the advantage of being at ease with others, even those they would have been uncomfortable to be with at an earlier time. When a teenager's self-esteem grows, it shows. They tend to be more relaxed and less challenged by unfamiliar faces. When a teenager sheds their insecurity, comfort and relaxation prevail along with self-confidence.

All it takes for a teenager to become a dynamo of achievement is self-confidence. When self-confidence is abundant, a teenager feels like they are on top of the world and can do anything they decide to do. Without self-confidence, a teenager tends to be fearful of moving forward and sputters instead of flying high.

Nearly every successful adult has passed through times of low self-confidence. There is only one way to overcome a self-confidence deficiency. Challenge yourself, first, on small things such as looking straight at the person who is speaking to you. Pay attention to what they are saying rather than focusing on feeling uncomfortable. When you pay close attention, you are likely to add a comment or ask a leading question that expands the conversation.

It feels good to be part of a conversation and uncomfortable to be on the sideline not engaging with others. Some people do not leave space for others to join the conversation preferring to showboat. They love the position of being the center of attention, and that is where their focus remains. They are more intent on hogging the spotlight than in relating positively with others. With this type of maneuvering, they tend to lose their audience.

Shy teenagers tend to be more quiet than outgoing teenagers are. Outgoing teenagers have a propensity to fit in wherever they go, whereas shy teenagers are often quietly figuring things out. Each person has their own comfort level to strive to maintain; however, it is highly beneficial for all teenagers to develop self-confidence.

A self-confident person adapts and adjusts to changing conditions by contributing when they can and honoring other people's contributions. People who dominate, dictate, and shine the spotlight on themselves are trying to create a glamorous persona, which is phony. Their attempt to be impressive has no correlation to their value. **The innate value of every person is the same. All people are precious and deserving of respect.**

Always extend to others the treatment that you would prefer to receive. Everyone enjoys receiving a smile or nod of approval from others. Sometimes individuals do not bother to consider how they come across to others, feeling entitled to express themselves with no reservations while disregarding their impact upon other people. Give yourself high standards of personal ethics, including the well-being of other people as being equal to your own well-being.

I hope you do not think that I am faulting you for being a typical teenager. My goal is solely to give you the path to becoming the best person that you can be. Now is your time to learn how to shine with outstanding traits that you can develop within yourself. Build strength of character and self-assurance will follow, enabling you to express yourself with confidence throughout the rest of your life.

A person develops self-confidence by experiencing success. Building success happens naturally, as a person puts forth their best effort to attend to their responsibilities. There are many kinds of responsibilities. First, you have the duty to yourself to express honorable traits and qualities such as truthfulness, dependability, and pitching in to assist when there is a need you can fill. These are the basic responsibilities.

Then there are responsibilities to home and family. Any organization requires joint effort to thrive, and this is especially true within families. Families who do not pull together to support and care for one another put a strain on every family member.

Especially during challenging times, pulling together builds strong character. Even if problems remain, the family will likely become closer and even more firm in their dedication to each other's well-being. Much good comes from a family's commitment to supporting each other.

Inner strength and good character result from one's determination to remain honest and ethical. If you want to build solid self-esteem, live your life with an eye toward maintaining a pristine code of ethics. Being a moral and ethical person builds a solid base for self-respect, which encourages one to feel good about themself.

Feeling good about oneself invigorates a person to step forward to try new things without being afraid of failure. Fear holds many people back from fully satisfying their ambitions. **One never knows what they are capable of accomplishing until they give it a go.** So take that all-important first step and give yourself the opportunity to succeed.

How you feel about yourself is of utmost importance. Your duty to yourself is to emphasize your positive traits while being aware of your lesser qualities, which need improvement. Do not make excuses for negligent or poor behavior. Excuses do not advance one's character development. If you want to build a better version of yourself, hold yourself to high standards of accountability.

Be kind and respectful to yourself and all people. Put a smile on your face instead of a frown, and appreciate those who contribute to your well-being. Instead of demanding more for yourself, be willing to give more of yourself to boost the well-being of other people.

The payoff for developing these attributes will show up immediately. Your self-esteem will flourish, as well as your self-confidence. You will find yourself at ease socially and not be afraid to speak up if you disagree with another person's point of view. You will be expressing yourself as a secure person who has self-confidence and respect for others.

To make the most of your life, give it your best shot as you go along. Every day is precious, filled with the potential to express yourself in your uniqueness. **Every person has special qualities, aptitudes, and tendencies.** Do not covet other people's gifts and traits. Instead, focus on your positive attributes and put them to work.

Perceive yourself and all others as sisters and brothers who are dear to each other. Treat all people with respect and consideration, and be patient when interacting with others. Do not expect other people to agree with your perceptions and do not feel that you should have to agree with theirs. Give your relationships breathing room for individual self-expression.

In general, people attract others who are similar to themselves. There is comfort and ease between people when they have a lot in common. However, when it comes time for marriage, many people find themselves attracted to their opposites.

You can guess what this brings about down the road. Couples must learn to handle living with someone who has their own opinions and ways of doing things. People are not ready for marriage until they become adept at compromising and valuing their spouse's preferences without surrendering their own.

Teenagers, do not blunder through your teenage years. Instead, express yourself with awakening maturity. You are on your way to becoming the person in charge of every aspect of your life.

Wise up. Look around and see what is right with the world and what is wrong. Start thinking about what you might do to help fix the problems in the world.

You do not have to carry this entire responsibility by yourself. Others will follow your lead, but your broad leadership is required to ignite public interest in participating. If your generation sputters and ignores poor decisions made by the older generations, there is little chance that our planet Earth will remain dependably stable and supportive for the human race.

Teenagers, your generation has the ability to generate deep concern for the viability of planet Earth among the older generations. It is up to you to take the reins of rationality and lead negligent others in the right direction. I urge you not to delay exhibiting a groundswell of determination to initiate protective steps to halt blatant disregard for your planetary residence.

Your planet requires champions to stand up for her, protect and preserve her and hold her with reverence. Unfortunately, there is no universal commitment to your planet's well-being. Some people, here and there, are deeply committed, others are somewhat committed, but most do not even recognize their responsibility to their planetary residence. The health and well-being of your planet take a back seat to other concerns such as feeding yourselves today. Immediate concerns take center stage while people fail to address long-term complications that will ultimately impact the well-being of everyone.

Planet Earth needs champions who care about her and are ready to go to bat for her. Every reasonable person's assistance is required. **Teenagers, you have the ability to rouse your generation to take on the cause of protecting and preserving planet Earth. You can accomplish what older generations have failed even to acknowledge – the necessity of safeguarding your planetary home so she will continue to allow humanity's residence upon her.**

One never knows what they are capable of accomplishing until they give it a go. So, take that all-important first step and give yourself the opportunity to succeed.

Teenagers,
you have the ability to rouse your generation to take on the cause of protecting and preserving planet Earth. You can accomplish what older generations have failed even to acknowledge – the necessity of safeguarding your planetary home.

CHAPTER SEVEN

MAKE GOOD CHOICES

Personal worlds taken together are what create our societies. Societies reflect the preferences and attitudes of their populations. In your school, you have become acquainted with students who reflect your background as well as students who come from backgrounds decidedly different from your own.

Do you want to expand your perceptions? Become acquainted with people who do not share your background or experiences. Extend yourself to those who may be of a different race or from different socio-economic circumstances.

Teenagers tend to gravitate to those who share the same background. Those who are openhearted go out of their way to include all others. Be aware that those who limit friendships to their lookalikes risk becoming stuck in a rut of narrowmindedness. They often fail to recognize the richness that comes with diversity.

Everyone deserves to enjoy respect from others without needing to puff themselves up to seem attractive. No one is comfortable when being excluded. Inclusion is of utmost importance.

People who are most genuine and caring draw others' attention in a soft, gentle way. Bring forth your authentic self-expression but keep an eye on how your expression affects other people. Do not become a person who considers themself as being more or less important than someone else is.

A good way to live one's life is to think of everyone else as your brother or sister. Think in terms of everyone being part of a big family that has unique and interesting people. Then acknowledge that you are a precious and important part of that family. Make an effort to foster healthy self-acceptance within yourself. Be sure not to hold yourself above or below other people.

Do not be blind to your shortcomings, but do not allow them to define who you are. If you think that perfection exists within the human race, you are mistaken. Every person has aspects that do not reflect the more positive side of themself.

If you pull the wool over your eyes and only focus on your positive aspects, you will lose the opportunity to become a better version of yourself. Taking the opposite track of wallowing in what you perceive as your negative aspects will park you in a big imbalance of perception. Instead, view your plusses and minuses with clear vision and determine to emphasize the positives while striving to eliminate the negatives.

Teenagers have vast potential tucked inside of them. Some of these potentials are readily apparent, but others seem to pop up at certain moments in time. When teenagers follow their positive instincts, they may be on the road to self-discovery.

Opportunities that come along may lead you to uncover some of your hidden potentials. Some people who are writers began by writing for their high school newspapers. Great chefs emerge from those whose interest in cooking began early in life. Participating in high school athletics may lead to playing professional sports or coaching. Choices and decisions made in high school may have a powerful impact on a teenager's future.

My sister, Louise, knew she wanted to become a nurse when she was four years old. She carried her doll tucked under her arm while announcing to family members that she was going to be a nurse. Louise became a pediatric nurse and worked for several years in a psychiatric hospital for adolescents. Her experience is an example of the inner knowing that some people have even when they are a child.

One's direction in life will come to them, and sometimes this happens sooner rather than later. Children display their interests even at a very early age. For example, a child I knew as a two-year-old enjoyed cooking. When his mother cooked dinner, he pulled out his special pot and wooden spoon and pretended to cook right alongside her. As an adult, he enjoys cooking as much as he did when he was a toddler.

It is important for teenagers to become aware of their interests and engage in them when possible. Identifying one's life calling may happen at any time. **By following your interests and your instincts, you are likely to create satisfying opportunities for yourself on the road of life.**

Teenagers are a beautiful gift to humanity. Filled with energy, vitality, and creativity, teenagers are open to approaching problem solving differently than older generations. Older generations were successful in bringing in their new ways, which were fitting and desirable. Nevertheless, there is always a need for new perceptions and creativity to improve what is now in place.

If the rest of humanity were more like teenagers, there would be more trying out new ideas, new approaches, and ultimately coming up with solutions that reflect thinking outside the box. Teenagers are risk-takers. They like to develop their own preferences, some of which older generations simply do not understand.

Older people may lose their desire to innovate. Mainly, older people tend to relax into what has been familiar to them and find comfort in that. Whereas the younger generations are eager to instill new perceptions, attitudes, and ideas.

I encourage all teenagers to value themselves for their resourcefulness. Every day, teenagers have the opportunity to stretch their capabilities. The teenage years are a time of assuming responsibility for developing oneself and for having a positive impact on other people. These years are also the time of enjoying life, playing sports, or undertaking part-time employment.

Being a teenager is like test driving cars. One can try whatever options they choose to investigate, knowing they do not have to remain with that possibility. If that one suits them, they can continue with that experience. If that option turns out not to be satisfying, they can go on to sample another.

Many teenagers are like jugglers. They juggle many activities and seem to enjoy them all. Juggle without sacrificing your other responsibilities. You do not want to be required to repeat a class because you were having so much fun that you let your school responsibilities slide.

As you go through life, it is a good idea to have priorities. Your first priority should be to take care of your physical body. Do not endanger your body through neglect, recklessness, or overindulgence.

Respect your body. Yours is the only body you will have, so keep it in good condition. Please do not assume that it is indestructible. Treat your body as the precious instrument that it is.

Many teenagers find fault with their body, wishing that it were more perfectly formed or more attractive. Instead of noticing what you do not like, I suggest that you spend one afternoon deliberately thanking your body for all it does for you. Keep in mind an attitude of gratitude, and place your body high on the list of what is important to you.

Cherish your teenage years and delight in your inner growth, as well as your outer growth. You will be utilizing your experiences to build ever-increasing confidence in yourself. Every appropriate choice you make builds character. Every time you turn away from poor choices that may seem inviting at the time, you validate your good judgment and improve the strength of your character.

Sometimes teenagers do stupid things. Some of these are harmless and good for a laugh. However, driving a car at exceedingly high speeds is looking for big trouble. High-speed driving far too often results in serious injury, arm or leg amputation, or worse yet, a fatality. No one would want to carry the burden of having caused another person's death. Respect yourself and your body, and value other people's well-being as much as your own.

Valuing other people, whether you like them or not, displays innate goodness. Those with good character respect and care about other people, all other people, and not only those similar to themselves. People naturally gravitate to those who share their interests and perspectives. Sometimes people learn more by spending time with others who are not like themselves. Other people's perspectives can bring an expansion of open-mindedness.

Open-minded people can put themselves in other people's shoes, thereby gaining a clearer understanding of others' perspectives. How often do you hear two people arguing when each does not clearly understand the other's position, and they are too stubborn to settle down enough to listen to what the other person has to say? How can there be a settling of differences without calm consideration of both sides of an issue?

Teenage years bring a major expansion of one's perspectives. Instead of carrying over childish viewpoints, thoughtful and progressive teenagers establish their own code of ethics. They want to do what is best and right for themselves and pitch in to be a positive member of their family and community. These teenagers are taking on a broader determination to be tomorrow's leaders.

By following your interests and your instincts, you are likely to create satisfying opportunities for yourself on the road of life.

The teenage years bring a major expansion of one's perspectives.

CHAPTER EIGHT

CAPTAIN YOUR OWN SHIP

———

Teenagers, open your hearts to other people. Instead of wondering what people think of you, focus on demonstrating respect for all others, those your age, as well as those younger or older. People are people. No one is more important than any other, but notice that there is a vast difference in how various people conduct themselves.

People who tend to be egotistical are looking for validation. If they were secure, they would not be trying to gain other people's attention through artificial means. Building one's self up to be a big shot is a reflection of insecurity. One who is secure has no impulse to go out of their way to make themself appear to be more important than any other.

My advice is to enjoy being your natural self. Evaluate your positive and negative aspects with an eye toward accuracy, and develop a determination to do away with those aspects that do not reveal your better characteristics. The true self shines through more brightly when one strives to do away with their lesser traits and behaviors. You may think that these less desirable characteristics are just part of who you are; however with effort and determination, you can shrink them until they fade away.

Every person can improve themself. However, if one is not interested in taking that most important step, they will miss performing a very rewarding exercise. Do you enjoy sameness? Most people prefer a bit of adventure. **The most self-rewarding adventure you can take is to become a more wholesome person than you already are.**

Your life going forward will change for the better with every improvement you implement. If you stick with it, you will create a ripple effect that becomes more and more satisfying, even on a daily basis. Another payoff is that you will enjoy being yourself more as you refine your attitudes and self-expression to reveal your inherent appeal.

Self-improvement is not going to be a speedy process. You will find yourself slipping back into your former patterns, which you thought you had eradicated. As they pop back up, do not become discouraged. Sometimes they have to be ground down to a pulp before they disappear entirely.

The payoff is worth the effort. It will be as if you have thrown a heavy load into a ditch to get rid of it, when you feel yourself becoming a better person. Lightness and joy will replace the heavy feelings of insecurity and self-doubt.

You are the master of yourself, and you can hold yourself as precious and unique even as you undergo self-evaluation and correction. Do not take a nosedive into self-castigation for not being faultless. Instead, search for the areas you need to bring into a better form and attend to them as they come to your awareness. You are working toward expressing yourself more wholesomely, and this is a reason to celebrate.

Do not worry about mistakes you may have made in the past. Living life is more like a trial and error experience than following a set of instructions to build something. **People are not robots, and we each follow our own path, succeeding and failing, picking ourselves up and then trying again.**

One may become discouraged that they have a long way to go to become a more resilient yet compassionate and supportive person. I suggest that you notice and celebrate your every effort to raise yourself up to a higher standard of self-expression. Pull yourself up by your own bootstraps and enjoy knowing yourself as a secure and confident person who is aware of their shortcomings and determined to overcome them.

The more effort you put into refining your self-expression, the more pleasing the results will be for you, as well as for your friends and family. When we have a sour attitude, we pull others down as well. Conversely, when we are joyful and easy to get along with, smiles of delight from others reflect their appreciation.

Those enamored with themselves to such an extent that they put themself on a pedestal are convinced of their superiority over others. Their assumption of being better than others is a display of character weakness. Only insecure people have a need to perceive themselves as more elevated than other people. Those who are well adjusted cherish themself and others equally.

The best way to go forward in life is with courage, resourcefulness, and open-mindedness, traits that lead to a bountiful harvest. With these three traits, a person is bound to be effective. Courage gives one confidence that they will be successful in their endeavors if they step forward and perform well. Resourcefulness shows initiative and a willingness to put effort into the undertaking. Open-mindedness keeps one alert to innovative opportunities.

All teenagers have these characteristics within their selves. If they do not discount their capabilities, they will harvest them by putting them to good use. There is no future in discounting one's capabilities, even if one's family or peers may not be encouraging.

Always consider yourself the captain of your own ship. Pay attention to potentially valid points another person may bring up and analyze how those points might affect your plans. Do not be blind to valid concerns but do not automatically be mowed down by them either. Instead, maintain a can-do attitude and a willingness to make necessary adjustments.

Once teenagers begin to experience success, their self-confidence kicks in, propelling them to expand their realm of possibilities. With self-confidence, teenagers will not be afraid to try new things. Trying something new can lead to very satisfying experiences. Imagine the joy a teenager feels after discovering an aptitude for music or art, after having had no expectations.

Within humanity are tremendous talents and desirable attributes distributed generously. Teenagers become aware of their innate capabilities by following their interests and by daydreaming. Did you know that daydreaming may enhance decision-making? Daydreaming is a way to figure things out hypothetically, somewhat like trying on a pair of shoes before purchasing them.

Playing sports, singing in a choir, or volunteering as a teacher's aide expands a teenager's school experience. If you want to feel appreciated, volunteer to assist when you see a need you can fill. Teenage years are an important time to broaden one's experience and areas of competence.

As teenagers branch out to include new endeavors, their self-confidence broadens. With blooming self-confidence, teenagers feel more empowered. Lingering feelings of insecurity tend to melt away. For those who try, their expanding self-assurance powers them forward.

Self-confidence raises a teenager's perception of themself. One holds their head higher, less intimidated by challenges, when one is self-confident. Rarely does a person experience great success without self-confidence. Conversely, a self-confident person can fail in their endeavor without losing their self-esteem. Their perception of themself does not bob around, going from positive to negative, with the plusses and minuses of their life.

As teenagers step forward to express their individuality, they open the door to experiencing deeper satisfaction. It is rewarding to gather one's courage and stand in front of a group of one's peers, sharing information that enlightens others. When you become a resource for other people, they will hold you in high esteem, further promoting your self-confidence. Self-confidence is an important trait to foster within yourself.

Self-confidence within a person enables them to step forward to take a leading role to accomplish whatever needs doing. Self-confident people trust that they can get a job done. Even if they are inexperienced, they have the determination to forge ahead, trusting they will figure out what will need to be done as they go along. Self-confidence propels a person forward to apply themself in new ways.

There is no reason for a person not to have self-confidence. Rarely do people come up short when they strive to do their best. Striving to do one's best nearly always produces more than was anticipated. When self-confident people come up short in one area of endeavor, they apply the lessons they learned to their next endeavor, and keep challenging themselves.

Self-confident people are not afraid of failing because they know they have next time to get it right. They focus on their success and utilize the lessons they learned from failures to improve their effectiveness going forward. They concentrate on building more and more competence within themselves.

Without adequate self-confidence, a person may be more likely to give up instead of making it a point to learn from their errors to build more proficiency within themself. For example, a toddler learning to walk falls often, but that does not keep them from repeatedly practicing until they learn to maintain their balance and stability. **Imagine the life that a toddler would have if they stopped trying to walk because they fell down and did not want to risk falling again.**

People are not robots,
and we each follow our own path,
succeeding and failing, picking
ourselves up and then trying again.

Self-confident people are not afraid
of failing because they know they
have the next time to get it right.
Imagine the life that a toddler
would have if they stopped trying to
walk because they fell down and did
not want to risk falling again.

Always consider yourself the
captain of your own ship.

CHAPTER NINE

BE POSITIVE AND UPBEAT

Teenagers, you have a bright, satisfying future ahead of you. Give yourself your full support. Erase any self-doubt you may be engaging in. Encourage yourself and become your own best friend.

You have everything you need within yourself. Your responsibility is to harvest your particular gifts and aptitudes, but first, you must identify them. If you are interested in a specific course for your life, evaluate the obvious positive and negative aspects. Be realistic and investigative.

Give yourself recognition for all the mountains you climbed on your way to becoming a teenager. You taught yourself to read, write, follow the rules and express yourself. Every year you challenged yourself to progress along the path to adulthood.

Consider how you expanded your vision of what is possible for you to do. During your younger years, you relied on your parents to take care of you. They were watchful and protective. Now you make more decisions for yourself. You have been developing good judgment.

Teenagers, you are becoming the leaders of tomorrow. You must evaluate the difference between right and wrong and be committed to standing up for what is right, just, and protective for all. Your generation will be responsible for maintaining peace in the world.

No one likes to be looked down on or made fun of. Be certain that you always employ fair-mindedness and respect for all other people. Do not discount the importance of any other person, and always interact with other people, as you would prefer that they interact with you. Do not place yourself or anyone else on a pedestal.

Be wary of individuals who glamorize themself while showing disdain for other people. Instead, be impressed with people who see others as their equals and respect them as such. Caring about the well-being of other people is a very sound and doable commitment to make; it is a wonderful trait to expand within one's self.

On your way to creating a good life for yourself, do not overlook opportunities to assist others. You will be doing yourself a favor, as well as them. If you want to feel good about yourself, extend yourself to aid another person.

Every time you reach out with your support to console a person who is having a hard time, encourage someone experiencing self-doubt, or cheer on another's achievements, you become a better person. One of your main goals in life ought to be making yourself into an honorable, compassionate and supportive person. **Your own sense of self-worth expands when you contribute to the well-being of others.**

Although teenagers sometimes feel awkward and unsure of themselves, they each have capabilities beyond their ability to perceive. Part of the fun in life comes from extending oneself to try something new with no expectations or fear of failure. Nothing ventured, nothing gained.

With open-mindedness and a bit of courage, many doors open. There are doors to performing, such as in plays, musical events, and athletics. Other doors include publishing, such as with school newspapers or yearbooks. Do not overlook opportunities to sing in choirs or play in a band. Enrich your school experience, interact with other students and express your creativity.

One does not have to be a straight-A student to be successful. Do not measure your worthwhileness by comparing yourself to others. Instead, get better acquainted with yourself, noticing your positive attributes without discounting them. Appreciate the natural gifts that you may have been downplaying as you focus on what you see as deficiencies in yourself.

Always respect yourself. Hold your head high and strive to be a moral, ethical person. This attitude is step one in the foundation of self–esteem. Then proceed to the next step. With self-esteem, you empower yourself to stretch further and go farther. You act as a support to yourself instead of pulling yourself down. Now you are on your way to flying higher and going farther than you previously thought you could.

Self-doubt is not entirely negative. If one does not use self-doubt to persecute themself, it may add to their effectiveness. A dash of self-doubt leads one to recheck their decisions. This simple act has led to implementing beneficial adjustments at a most opportune time.

The best way to proceed is to go forward becoming the best version of yourself. Do not castigate yourself for every mistake you make. Do not ignore your missteps; be cognizant of them, but do not allow them to pile up as a heavy load that you continue to carry.

Become self-aware and self-correcting. Being self-correcting can get you to the top of the mountain behaviorally. Losing any self-deceptiveness a person has engaged in is freeing as if a heavy burden simply disappeared.

Every person has a responsibility to themself to take the high road in life, even when the high road becomes bumpy at times. Do not let yourself off the hook of accountability when tempted. Especially when honestly and integrity are involved, be unbending in your resolve to maintain your high moral and ethical standards.

Individuals build societies. Be an individual who contributes to the well-being of all other people, not only certain selected ones. Some people are more appealing than others, but all are important. People are like pieces of a puzzle. Each person is unique, and even when similar to another, they are not identical.

Be a person who is congenial, open-minded, and welcoming to others without choosing who deserves cordiality. Everyone enjoys a warm welcome and respect extended to them. Grumpy people are a nuisance, which infringes on other people's peace of mind, as well as their own. Train yourself to live on the sunny side of the street. You will enjoy being a positive, upbeat person.

Be a problem-solver, a person who takes responsibility for solving problems. Focus on your own difficulties. Leave other people's challenges for them to manage. Too often, people assume they are experts in knowing what other people should do. Keep your own house in order, and do not try to straighten out another person's house unless invited to do so.

Do not underrate yourself. Refrain from glamorizing other people and wishing you were more as they are. Recognize your attributes that are solid such as dependability, being true to your word, and respecting all other people. Step aside from conflicts. Leave space for other people's perspectives, respecting them even when they differ from your own.

Becoming a confident person requires self-approval for the right reasons. Achieving a goal that requires you to strive harder and stretch further is a reason for self-acknowledgment. Going beyond your expectations when participating in a spelling bee or another classroom exercise raises one's self-perception.

Nudge yourself along to test your expanding skills and be pleased with yourself.

Concentrate on the positive side of life. Do not be mowed over by life's challenges. Turn negatives into positives when you can and take good care of yourself. You are precious, unique, and deserving of appreciation and respect.

Hold your head high with confidence and set out to be your best self. Give yourself acknowledgment and appreciation when you notice the positive transformation that is taking place within you. When you gather in a group with other people, you will be more at ease expressing yourself, and your shortcomings will not bother you as much as they did.

If you have had a tendency to shine a spotlight on yourself, you will notice that urge diminished. You will become more cognizant of the value of other people's perspectives and more interested in hearing other points of view. The natural next step is becoming a better team player. Instead of striving for your own glory, you will be pleased when you contribute to a group effort.

Teenagers have the opportunity to establish a firm foundation for the rest of their life. By striving to live day-to-day being an honest, participating member of society, one prepares themself to make well thought out choices for themselves in the future. By considering the well-being of other people to be as important as their own well-being, one displays their integrity.

Give yourself recognition for all the mountains you climbed on your way to becoming a teenager. Every year you challenged yourself to progress along the path to adulthood.

By considering the well-being of other people to be as important as their own well-being, one displays their integrity.

CHAPTER TEN

FOCUS ON SELF-IMPROVEMENT

—

Teenagers, together you can advance civilization. Every generation ties in with prior generations, first learning from them and then carrying civilization to a more advanced level, unless a powerful force for evil such as Adolph Hitler becomes their leader. Never give credibility to a person who convinces other people to hurt harmless individuals.

Every person is entitled to respect and safety. In an ideal world, hurtfulness, disrespect, and incivility would no longer exist. Humanity needs good role models who set their standards of behavior based on how they would like to be treated. So far, no particular generation has stepped forward to become the impetus for modeling ideal human behavior. Now it is your turn. May you be more successful than your predecessors were.

Your first step is to consider every other person as a member of a most precious family. This family appears to be unrelated; the members do not look like each other or act like each other. However, underneath outward appearances, they have the same life purpose. Each person's purpose is to advance their individual self-expression to further their evolutionary development.

Discord and conflict arise as people see things differently and value themself more than others. There is benefit in seeing things differently. Nearly everyone's perception has value, although some more than others. When considering all angles, more advanced perspectives come to light, more awareness prevails. Then better decisions will be identified.

Delete from your reasoning any form of self-elevation over others. Be rational and search out your own shortcomings. Address them and leave it to the others to deal with their own shortcomings. Every person can advance their self-expression by focusing on self-improvement.

Let go of whatever bothers you about other people. Relax your focus on other people's insufficiencies. If you cannot control your aggravation, do not blame them. Blame yourself.

There is a line between noticing other people's insufficiencies without judgment and judging their deficiencies as an indictment against them. Do not bother to judge other people. People judging other people does not bring improvement to anyone's self.

Train yourself to acknowledge other people's admirable qualities. Then, decide to develop these within yourself. When one becomes a better person, their self-esteem rises. It feels good to be an honorable person.

When you begin this process of advancing your perceptions and behaviors, you may feel as if you are attempting to climb a mountain. Keep climbing until you reach your peak performance, and then climb a little more. Everyone can do better than they may anticipate.

Sometimes you will delight yourself. Other times you will be disappointed. Leave self-criticism off the table. Focus on accurate self-evaluation. Whatever you do, make this exercise strictly about yourself. Do not use other people's behavior as an excuse for your mishandling of any situation.

Bit by bit, over time and with considerable effort, you will perceive improvements in your perceptions, attitudes, and responses to life's challenges. You will feel more satisfied within yourself. You will detect less dissatisfaction with others and find that you can let go of things that used to bother you.

Human beings have the power to make themselves better than they have been, or worse. When people behave instinctively, they often do not consider how they could have had a more effective response. Halt any instinct to react without first thinking about the consequences of your actions. Become a person who deliberates instead of acting impulsively. Choose your attitudes and responses, and do not allow them to fly out of you instinctively.

Teenagers represent humanity's best hope for a better tomorrow; however, few teenagers view themselves that way. Teenagers have a tendency to discount their importance. Although some teenagers are more confident than others, overall, most teenagers feel somewhat wobbly and insecure.

Teenagers have yet to discover their personal power. Personal power comes from within when a person respects themself. A person who is self-assured for the right reasons naturally generates self-respect.

Teenagers develop self-confidence when they set a goal and then work mightily to achieve that goal. Most teenagers are more capable than they realize. They may subdue their ambitions because they think they may not be good enough to be successful. Every person has talents and capabilities of which they are unaware. That potential will go unrealized if the person is afraid to give it a go.

Have you heard the adage "Nothing ventured, nothing gained"? This means that if you do not try, you will not achieve. People willing to attempt new endeavors open doors to success. **Typically, if a person has an aspiration to pursue a new endeavor, they are likely to enjoy participating in it.**

Every person has an inner compass. Those who consult their inner compass have the advantage of navigating to what is right for them to do. When a person keys into their inner compass, they receive accurate information. This inner compass leads one in the right direction.

In order for one's inner compass to work, one must set aside doubt of its validity. Doubt skews results. One's inner compass does not try to please. It merely renders results, which lead the person forward in their best direction.

Your inner compass is your best friend tucked inside of you. If you pay attention to it, you will make more sound decisions for yourself. To be successful in life, tap into your inner direction finder, which will give you the impulse to make decisions that are in your best interest and harmless to others.

Sometimes people make decisions solely based on what is best for them. In some instances, those decisions affect other people in negative ways. Keep in mind how your actions affect other people, and factor their well-being into your decision. Be a considerate and honorable person.

When a person holds themself to high standards of morals and ethics, something wonderful happens. Their self-respect grows. They gain more confidence in themselves. Then they tend to relax into self-confidence, which is a wholesome change for many people. When one has high standards and morals, they reach a pinnacle of achievement.

People tend to judge other people by their outward appearances. Outward appearances are irrelevant when determining the quality of a person. People with high standards, morals, and ethics stand out from their peers for their willingness to step up to support other people. These people are heroes. They live their lives with an eye to going out of their way to assist someone in need.

People helping other people is the humane and decent way to live. A successful life includes heartfelt caring for others. If a person wants to build their self-esteem, they will find that going out of their way to be of assistance to another person will give them self-esteem. Helping other people warms both people's hearts and boosts their self-esteem.

People are important and valuable regardless of their circumstances. Everyone has something to contribute to the progression of the human race. Every person adds to the evolution of humanity, which is taking place at a much slower pace than it could be.

Without an impetus to become more humane, compassionate, and inclusive, many people meander through their lifetimes; rigid, hurtful behaviors do not subside. Individuals undermining the well-being of certain others continue to interfere in the well-being of minorities, people of color, disabled individuals, and anyone else who is vulnerable to their harassment.

If your goal is to become a successful person in life, be sure to emphasize the well-being of other people. Any person who discounts the importance of another person is coming from a place of insecurity. People grounded in the delusion that they have a right to interfere in anyone else's well-being are insecure and poor representatives of humanity's potential to care about every other person.

There is only one person you can change. Do not attempt to remold any other person. Place your priority on bringing out the best in yourself. Identify your strengths and your weaknesses. Congratulate yourself for your strengths, and determine to eliminate, or at least decrease, your lesser traits. Pat yourself on the back when you identify progress. Be patient and give yourself time but do not take a vacation from your commitment to become a more evolved person.

People are important
and valuable regardless of their
circumstances.

There is only one person you can
change.

CHAPTER ELEVEN

FAIR AND EQUAL TREATMENT

—

When you look at yourself, what do you think? Do you think you are better than other people? Do you look at every fault you have and demean yourself? These are two traits, which are common among many people. Yet, both of these perceptions are inaccurate.

All people have imperfections. In addition, all people have goodness within themself, innate goodness. Some people's goodness shows quite clearly. They are eager to go about their life demonstrating their caring for others.

Our world is awash with hesitancy to tap into one's inner goodness. All too frequently, people's inner goodness remains dormant. Even as the world spins into disrespect for more and more people, there is no united effort to push back against the ill-treatment of those being targeted.

Every person is worthy of respect, even those who have poor instincts and qualities. Certain people do not present the better side of themselves. Nonetheless, they deserve fair and equal treatment. Everyone deserves fair and equal treatment.

If every person held the high standard of regarding all people as worthwhile, our world would become more benevolent. People would actually feel better about their selves. Most people have some insecurity. Judging the worthwhileness of any other person indicates that one has not learned to regulate his or her own insecurities.

Living life as a human being can lead a person to the greatest heights of achievement or to the prison door. Everyone directs their own path. Teenagers benefit when they slow down to consider the ramifications of their intentions before acting. It is always best to steer away from any form of dishonesty, hurtfulness, or lowering of your standard of conduct. Do not go downhill when raising your behavior is the objective.

You have the opportunity to know yourself as a very worthwhile person or as a troublemaker. Troublemakers may delight in causing disruption, feeling successful when they do. Unless their disregard for another's well-being boomerangs back against them, they feel empowered. Those who manipulate to cause discomfort to another person are asking for trouble.

There is a law of karma, which reveals that what goes around comes around. This means that a person, who deliberately instigates to bring harm to another person, will pay for their injustice by experiencing the same pain and suffering they caused the person they disrupted. Only create positive impacts. Protect your own well-being by reigning in any instinct to interfere in another person's life in a negative manner.

Live on the positive side of life. Go out of your way to exercise your positive aspects. Live honorably. Lend a helping hand when you notice someone in need of assistance. Do not bother to pat yourself on the back or take a bow for performing a good deed. Let this be your normal behavior and not something out of the ordinary.

There is nothing more rewarding than developing self-esteem, not for what you have but for what you do to assist people. Self-esteem generated by being helpful grows with every act of kindness. Becoming a noble member of the human race builds self-confidence and self-respect.

Teenagers are a tremendous resource for humanity. From them will come fresh ideas and solutions to lingering problems. Teenagers learn that older generations rarely move swiftly to implement necessary improvements within society. Instead of moving forward with much-needed improvement, older generations seem content with the way things are, especially in how people treat each other.

People tend to reflect their upbringing when relating to other people. Those, who did not witness their parents and other family members enjoying friendships with people of different backgrounds and races, initially may not be comfortable forming such relationships. Typically, when they do extend their respect and friendship, they are welcomed. Connections, which would not have otherwise occurred, blossom.

Teenagers sometimes have narrow parameters. They have not yet gained enough life experience to know that there is complexity, uniqueness, and great beauty within every person. Expansion of perception takes place as teenagers form friendships with others who do not come from their same background.

Every person faces many crossroads during their life. Crossroads are like street corners. They offer each person a choice of which direction to choose. If one selects the wrong direction, they end up taking an unnecessary detour.

Teenagers who avoid the low road of disparaging behavior exhibited toward some other people have higher self-esteem. By being openhearted toward others, they experience a greater sense of self-worth, which builds self-confidence. Kindness to others pays off personally and nurtures oneself.

With self-respect and confidence, people step forward in life invigorated and willing to try harder to accomplish their goals. They do not give up trying if their initial intentions do not pan out well. Instead, they reevaluate, make adjustments and then power forward.

Unless you stay on track and keep working to create the outcome you desire, you will achieve less than you could have. Do not short-change yourself. Set reasonable goals for yourself and then step forward to achieve them.

Every time you set an objective for yourself and then accomplish that objective, you expand your perception of what you are able to achieve. Be sure you are realistic. Choose goals that are attainable giving yourself the opportunity to experience success.

People who live their life simply, reacting to what happens rather than deliberately deciding what they intend to do, bob along instead of plowing forward. Some people meander their way through life and then wonder why their life does not feel satisfying. Set goals and aspirations for yourself. You are the only one who can determine your ambitions and fulfill them.

Having confidence in yourself propels you forward. Desire and determination ultimately get you to your destination. Do not hesitate to reach high and go far. It is up to you to bring out the best in yourself and put it to work.

Teenagers, do not discount your importance. You are humanity's children who hold the future in your hands. Ultimately, you will lead, and other generations will follow. Now is the time to begin to take responsibility for improving interpersonal relationships with all other people.

Do not judge another person's value by the color of his or her skin. Instead, display warmth and respect to all others and especially treasure the differences between people. Those, who do not look alike, think alike, or act alike, add richness to everyone's experiences.

If everyone in the world felt love and respect for all other people, humane treatment of all people would become normal behavior. People would be more inclined to work together for the good of all, and everyone would benefit. Our world does not have to remain conflict-bound and disparaging to minorities. We can do better, but some people must step forward to lead the rest.

People often play follow-the-leader. Even those who understand the importance of fair treatment for all individuals may abandon their position when pressed to do so by those in leadership without a moral compass. Stay away from disrespectful people who do not value all people equally.

Hold to your own decision to honor and respect people from all walks of life, including those from differing nationalities and socio-economic backgrounds. You will find much in common with people who are decidedly different from you. Those differences will show you many wondrous aspects of humanity.

Being convinced of one's superiority is a mistake that insecure people commonly make. Only an insecure person would attempt to boost their self-esteem by devaluing any other person. Well-balanced people have no urge to diminish the importance of others.

Hold your head high. Respect yourself and every other person, as well. When you take this step, your self-esteem will flourish. You will feel good about yourself. Your self-confidence will increase as you feel warmth from those who respond to your friendliness.

People who step onto the sunny side of life bring others along with them. How enjoyable it is to relax with friends and new acquaintances enjoying each other's company. Like attracts like.

You will attract those who share your good nature when you extend yourself to welcome newcomers into your circle of friends.

Create a satisfying life for yourself by utilizing your strengths while building new ones. Here are some valuable strengths to instill within oneself. Dependability is at the top of the list, followed by honesty and the commitment to be true to your word. If you commit to doing something, follow through. Be a person that others can rely upon. Building good character and sound relationships go hand in hand.

Honesty, reliability, and integrity are what life is all about. Those who develop these and other honorable traits will experience great satisfaction in their lives. If you want to be a person who feels good about themself, take the high road in life. Respect other people and do what you can when you see a need you can fill.

Teenagers are a tremendous resource for humanity. From them will come fresh ideas and solutions to lingering problems.

Having confidence in yourself propels you forward. Desire and determination ultimately get you to your destination.

Hold to your own decision to honor and respect people from all walks of life, including those from differing nationalities and socio-economic backgrounds.

CHAPTER TWELVE
EMPOWER YOURSELF

Teenagers, it is time for you to get to know yourself, not as a beginner but as a person picking up steam as you go along maturing your outlook on life. You have passed the awkward years and will soon be developing a clearer picture of what your future might look like if you have not already started to do so. You are about to make choices, which will affect you in the years ahead.

Have you identified your particular strengths and weaknesses in the classroom? What are your favorite subjects? Do you daydream about a certain occupation? Do not worry if you have not been inclined in that direction yet.

I ask these questions to alert you to the necessity to know yourself at a deeper level than you may have before. In the future, you will decide how to proceed with your life. You may not need to make any decisions immediately, but it helps to start thinking about your future without the pressure of making an immediate choice without expansive consideration of your options.

When you daydream about your future, what comes up for you? Pay attention. Do not necessarily dismiss an occupation that may seem unobtainable. Tap into your heart's desire, and then go for it. If you are still in the uncertain stage, mentally try out your interest areas. Imagine what a particular path might look like and how it might feel.

Determine if you might feel drawn to inventing products, working in other forms of business, or fields such as medicine or education. Some people instinctively know their best occupational fit whereas, others have varied interests and have trouble identifying one in particular. The simple act of becoming aware of occupational options has the potential to identify an appealing fit.

Certain occupations have specific background requirements. However, do not press yourself if you have no particular area of interest at this point. At the right time, you will gain awareness of what appeals to you, and then you will be going in the right direction as you investigate your options.

Teenagers, stay grounded in the present but look toward the future. Do not set up any roadblock that will keep you from creating a satisfying future for yourself. Know yourself, your interest areas, and your aptitudes. Apply yourself in your studies and give yourself opportunities to advance your ambitions.

Stay the course. Do not lose faith in yourself if challenging situations arise. You can utilize tough circumstances to strengthen yourself. Do not allow anyone to interfere with your well-being. Those who initiate hurtfulness against another person are trying to raise their self-esteem by being intimidating.

Empower yourself. Keep yourself strong in spirit, will, and determination. An empowered person is less likely to be bowled over by bullies. A show of strength carries weight, especially with those who are intimidating. Defeat intimidation with actions designed to shore up your own defenses. React decisively. Summon authorities if need be.

Go through life knowing that you are important. Do not think of yourself as being of lesser importance than any other person.

One does not need special credentials to be entitled to civil, humane treatment from all other people.

Always treat other people with respect and courtesy, which tends to uplift oneself as well as those with whom you interact. Be patient. Simple patience pays good dividends. It is not difficult to establish these traits within yourself when you decide to direct your efforts in this direction.

Life is full of lessons to learn and beneficial attitudes and behaviors to establish within oneself. When we step forward knowing that we are capable of refining our attitudes and actions to reflect our finer aspects, we are on our way to becoming better people than we have previously been. From this beginning, we can set our objective to advance even further. Perfection may be out of our reach, but we can come closer than we have before.

Each of us can become a more kind and caring person than we have been, but only when we set this objective as our goal. If we do not strive to refine our rough spots, they will not smooth out and disappear. Our efforts are required, and we will know they are effective when we become more caring and considerate. What may have begun as an effort will become a joyful awakening to the better side of ourselves.

Every step a person takes to express the better aspects of humanity will provide that person with invigorated self-confidence. People feel good about themselves when they behave honorably. Self-esteem comes from performing up to a high level. The highest level for every person is to honor and respect all other people.

Every person has the capability to express themself honorably and with respect toward all others. Be a person who lives by these standards. You will feel good about yourself as your self-esteem expands and your confidence builds. The better you feel about yourself, the more success you will have going forward in your life.

Know yourself as someone gifted with an opportunity to express your unique talents and abilities. Believe in yourself. Be your own best friend and choose what is best and right for yourself.

Do not compare yourself to other people. Each person is different from all others. Your goal is to discover those areas which particularly interest you. Your interests will lead you forward, especially when determining the choices you will make as you advance your education.

Think about today but with an eye focused on tomorrow. You will want to be a good person, one who chooses moral, ethical conduct. Use this as your foundation, and then build your life choices.

Get to know yourself with thoughtful attention to identifying your true nature. Every person has sparkling qualities along with qualities that are not advantageous. Do not lean on your objectionable traits and behaviors. Target them for removal.

You will be freeing yourself from anchoring in poor self-expression. Every person has a choice. Have you heard the term *take the high road*? The high road refers to the honorable path. Taking the high road leads to satisfaction with oneself.

When a person takes the high road, they commit to behaving with respect shown to all others, kindness and empathy extended, especially to those experiencing difficulties, and eagerness to help people needing assistance. In times of distress, those who step forward to put supportive arms around a person who is experiencing hardship display the better side of humanity. Every person has the potential to take the high road in life.

Part of a person's education comes from book learning and lectures. Another very important part is learning to be sensitive to how you treat other people. A good technique to employ is to consider every person as your dear sister or brother. One does not have to be related to another person in order to consider them a sister or brother. All of humanity is related.

The urge to hurt another person stems from poor self-esteem and a need to demonstrate superiority. Nothing good comes to either person when one acts against the well-being of another person. An innocent person takes the hit while the instigator suffers the loss of their humanity.

There are ways to overcome poor self-esteem. Hold your head high and determine to behave commendably. Self-esteem builds with every kindness you extend, every moral and ethical choice you make, and every smile you share with others. Gently notice a lessening of insecurities as you practice these three steps consciously until they become your natural choice of expression.

Every person has value, even those who trip themselves up with unwholesome behavior. Respect all people and assist when you can. Sometimes those displaying distressing behavior are crying out for someone to draw close to them, befriend them, and extend the support that they do not receive from other sources.

Always value yourself and conduct yourself with wholesome attitudes and behaviors. Care about the well-being of those who encounter more difficulty in their lives. Let your heart show. Be kind, considerate, and gracious to all others.

The payoff for instilling these characteristics within yourself is high self-concepts. You will feel confident, self-assured, and eager to press on with life, knowing that you will succeed. You will also find a broadening desire to be of assistance to those who need a helping hand or a friend to stand by their side.

All people have the opportunity to extend a helping hand to those who need assistance. By simply attuning yourself to the difficulties that some people endure and determining to help them, opportunities to assist will become apparent. When this happens, press forward and do what you can to demonstrate your concern for their well-being.

Helping others gives one's self-esteem a big boost. Help yourself to a big serving of self-esteem by making it a practice to be kind and thoughtful in your interactions with other people. Keep a positive attitude and watch it spread to your companions.

Always treat other people with respect and courtesy, which tends to uplift oneself as well as those with whom you interact.

Think about today but with an eye focused on tomorrow. You will want to be a good person, one who chooses moral, ethical conduct. Use this as your foundation, and then build your life choices.

CHAPTER THIRTEEN
BEHAVIORAL STANDARDS

Teenagers, what makes a good person? Have you thought about this question before? What are your parameters for determining who is a good person? Most people would agree that a good person is someone who cares about other people and goes out of their way to help someone in need of assistance.

Good people abide by sound moral and ethical considerations. They are rational in their responses to challenging situations and do not surrender fair-mindedness to gain the upper hand. Those who jockey for the upper hand may be more interested in self-advancement than in extending themselves to assist others.

Give assistance freely. Then when you require assistance, do not be hesitant to accept help from other people. People helping other people is what makes the world a better place for all to reside.

Teenagers, it is not too soon for you to learn the basics of being an admirable person. As you live more years of your life, you will appreciate what others do to assist you as you go along. Sometimes you will be the one that others depend upon to help them. People helping other people is the gold standard for living a commendable life.

Teenagers sometimes deal with indecision. They see some people expressing themselves rudely without caring whose feelings they hurt. They see other people being kind and considerate. If you do not develop an inclination to choose the higher road, you may be inclined to experiment with expressing your baser instincts.

Baser instincts are those compulsions, which do not represent the better side of humanity. When people give in to their baser instincts, disregard for the well-being of other people comes to the forefront. This is when discrimination often rears its ugly head. Discrimination is a vile compulsion within certain segments of humanity. Discrimination voids common decency.

Treat all people as you want others to treat you. This is a golden rule that is not honored, as it should be. Teenagers, do not fall into the same behaviors that you see thrust upon those who are discriminated against.

Stand up for those who carry the burden of discrimination. Omit from your mind and your heart any assumption that one group of people is superior or inferior to another. Take the viewpoint that all people are precious and worthwhile.

Teenagers, take the higher road in life and persuade older generations to follow your example. Older generations made some improvements during their lifetimes, but more improvements are necessary for the world to become a humanitarian place for all people to reside. Unfortunately, the human race is self-absorbed. People value themselves above all, even when they rely on each other and their planet to provide what they need.

There are two ways for people to learn. The first way to learn is by paying attention to knowledgeable people. The other way to learn is by disregarding experts, thereby setting themselves up to experience the predicted results.

Unfortunately for the common good, those who warn about the necessity to take precautions to protect the integrity of planet Earth's viability for upcoming generations do not have enough people's attention. Mostly they are ignored. Not enough concern for our Earth's well-being will result in her continuing to threaten us with toxic environmental issues, viruses that rage out of control, and inadequate food supplies.

Teenagers, you have a responsibility to stand firm in the protection of your planet's natural resources. Do not give in to big businesses that only care about moneymaking. They take their money and run. Instead, fight against those who disregard your planet's well-being by shunning their products in the marketplace.

When teenagers unite for a good cause, they flex their muscles in a positive way. Teenagers, your opinions are important. Do not think that your ideas are insignificant. Many times, teenagers readily catch on to better ways to do things. When adults pay attention to teenagers' opinions and suggestions, they are more likely to update their own perceptions.

Teenagers show the way to tomorrow. If it were not for teenagers, the way things are would remain static. Life would be dreary with sameness. New ideas come from fresh thinking, changing preferences, and adventuresome attitudes. Businesses delight in catering to teenagers' desires for innovations.

Teenagers have choices to make. The most meaningful option is to live a life of honesty, integrity, and concern for the well-being of all people. When teenagers stand tall in support of minorities, they serve as their elders' teachers. They model appropriate behavior, which some within the older generations may be inclined to ignore.

Teenagers will set the standards for future generations. Together they can revise today's misperceptions regarding the importance of supporting the well-being of every person. No person is insignificant. Life circumstances may lead some to choose undesirable behavioral options, which does not excuse reprehensible behavior but shows cause for it.

The best thing for our world is for teenagers to unite to raise the standards of treatment for all people. Teenagers have the most to gain by improving behavioral standards across the

board. They will ensure that they will live in a more gracious and accepting world and raise their children in a more uniformly positive environment than they may have experienced.

The world is an unwelcoming place for those who do not match their neighbors. When a neighborhood consists of a certain race of people, and then a family of a different race moves in, they are likely to be ignored. However, those who are congenial will welcome all people and treat everyone with courtesy and respect.

All people have the potential to be warm and gracious to all other people. Do not assume that a person of a different race or nationality is inferior or superior to any other person. Good qualities in a person do not correlate with ethnicity or nationality.

Be an open-minded, caring person whose heart remains receptive to people of all nationalities. Celebrate others' presence in your life and learn from them. Enrich your own life by including people from other backgrounds than your own.

Narrow-minded people limit their interest in those who differ from themselves. However, if they overcome that hurdle, they open the door to many forms of enjoyment. Learning from those who offer new perspectives can be stimulating and thought-provoking.

People, who hold themselves as being superior to other people, have a problem with low self-esteem. Low self-esteem is also present in those who consider themselves inferior to other people. It is common for those with poor self-esteem to strive to impress other people by coming on strong or as a big shot. Big shots puff themselves up with hot air, which deflates when others are no longer impressed with their maneuvers.

People who are humble in their self-presentation are admirable. They are satisfied being who they are. Their genuineness invites others to enjoy being with them. Arrogant people try to be impressive but have less to offer than they attempt to convey.

Model yourself after those you admire. There are many good role models. One thing they have in common is caring for and respecting all other people, especially those who do not have many advantages in life. Admire people who support the underprivileged populations and then provide any additional assistance you can.

Build your self-esteem through acts of kindness and caring extended to those who need support. Treat all others graciously and never look down on an impoverished person. Instead, be grateful for the opportunity to assist them.

Recognize other people's feelings and do what you can to help others when they are feeling down and out. Patiently listen to them when they want to talk about their problems. Be encouraging but refrain from telling other people what they should do. Let them choose their path forward.

Do for others what you would appreciate if the tables were turned and you were the person with overwhelming life challenges. Gently present potential options the other person could consider to ease their burdens. Above all, avoid an air of superiority and do not start preaching.

When hard times hit, the future looks bleak, and sometimes we make them worse because of our despair. During these times, people tend to appreciate a conversation with someone who truly cares about their well-being. Do not think that you can solve another person's problems, but listen intently in case you have something of value to suggest to them.

Teenagers, rise up together to demonstrate compassion, love, and kindness to the world. Practice these commendable attributes with each other and make them part of your natural way of being. Teaching others by example is far more effective than any other approach.

Teenagers,
you have a responsibility to stand
firm in the protection of your
planet's natural resources. Do not
give in to big businesses that only
care about moneymaking. They take
their money and run. Instead, fight
against those who disregard your
planet's well-being by shunning
their products in the marketplace.

The best thing for our world is
for teenagers to unite to raise the
standards of treatment for all
people.

CHAPTER FOURTEEN

HONOR AND RESPECT ALL PEOPLE

——

Humanity at its finest reflects nobility. There are different kinds of nobility. Kings and queens, considered royals, are obvious examples of nobility. Then there are people who achieve nobility because they conduct themselves with honor and goodness. They initiate wholesome interactions with other people.

Every person, although not a king or queen, is capable of expressing themself honorably. However, most people are not particularly strict with their self-expression. Their self-expressions may be instinctive, being delivered instantaneously without prior thought. Many people speak out of line, not realizing the hurtful nature of what they are saying, even as they hear their own words spoken.

Being too quick to jump in with a comment can create an avoidable mishap. Those who make it a point to consider their response before blurting it out are more likely to avoid making an offensive comment. Well-thought-out responses are more likely to be respected and carefully considered.

People who care about other people monitor their effect on others. They reign in any urge to be combative or objectionable. They would rather hold themselves back from hurting another person's feelings than going ahead with knee-jerk reactions, which others would find disheartening. When people care about others, they treat them as they would like to be treated. Caring for others warms people's hearts and opens doors to deeper relationships.

When a person starts their day, typically, they think about what they expect to accomplish during that day. Many set a plan for themselves. Planning helps keep a person focused on what is most important at that time.

Make a plan consisting of your main objectives for your life. Most people are interested in three things: career success, adequate or above adequate income, and possessions. Although these are some main components of a fulfilling life, successful people include another element.

I suggest that you include a determination to advance your appreciation of, and respect for, every person you encounter. Do not allow any impression to overturn civility, even-mindedness, and human decency. Always interact with others in a way that reflects the more evolved aspects of humanity.

There is a golden rule that states *always treat other people as you would prefer to be treated*. If you do not deviate from this instruction, you will be a commendable person. Be a responsible citizen and create a positive example. When more and more people reflect outstanding attitudes and behaviors, their impact will extend outward. This will bring rationality and kindness into people's minds, hearts and actions.

When a person interacts beneficially with all other people, that person is expanding their enjoyment of life. Life's burdens lighten when people refine their attitudes and behaviors. Extended relaxation and peacefulness occur when one avoids self-induced agitation brought on by criticizing others.

Some people believe that our world is going in an improper direction. Many attitudes and actions obviously undermine civility and respect. However, typically behind the scenes of the world's disturbances, many decent, loving, caring people quietly go about living their honorable lives. These are the people to imitate.

When our world turns in the wrong direction, much disruption and hurtfulness prevail. **During such times, it is of imperative importance for decent people to stand up for basic humanitarianism. Lead with your determination to honor and respect all people and their rights as human beings.**

There is another aspect of humanity that requires attention. Although most people criticize mentally, if not openly, what other people do, most people gloss over their own lesser traits. While another person's transgressions may repeatedly play upon a person's mind, people normally allow their own behavioral deficits to escape their focus.

When they set out to assess behaviors, most people focus on other people rather than themselves. They have clearer perception when viewing others' faults than when viewing their own shortcomings. People spend endless time mentally criticizing others' behaviors as if they had none of their own that needed improvement.

Keep in mind that each person is the captain of his or her own ship. No one has the capability of altering another person's self-expression. Even when a person's self-expression is destructive, rarely will another person's intervention change that person's choice of expression.

However, do not sit idle if certain people set out to undermine another person's well-being. Begin by summoning authorities, the obvious first action to take. You can attempt to attract others to align with you to create a distraction until police arrive.

When people disagree with each other, personal rights may be disregarded. When each side is convinced of their correctness and refuses to consider the other side's argument, no one gravitates to a middle ground. When this occurs, disagreements continue to fester.

If every person had the opportunity to set rules to be fair to all people, few would succeed if they had not received an education in what constitutes fairness to all. Nearly every person slants their perception to favor their objectives. Few people have the capacity to act independently from their personal motivations.

Being fair to all people has only one meaning. The term *fair to all people* connotes the same rules, regulations, and consequences for every person. You may ask yourself if the state of our world reflects fairness to all people. Few people would agree that it does.

Do you choose to establish better standards of behavior for humanity at large? Teenagers, this may seem like a heavy burden, but you are the ones with the capability to set more uniformly supportive standards for all people. Do not relax into the way things have been. Take it upon yourselves to update perceptions of how to treat others and what constitutes fairness to all.

Teenagers, are you ready to lead people to realign their thinking and attitudes? This is your time to act. Do not think for a minute that today's world will become a more fair and humane place for all people without your leadership.

I suggest you address these areas immediately. **Place loving arms around all people. Especially include people of differing races. Never discount the importance of any person. Hold every person as precious and respect all, always. In time, your ways will influence society's perceptions and behaviors.**

Every person has a part to play. Teenagers, take the lead and direct your efforts to the betterment of humanity. Step forward with protective arms around minority populations, in particular.

Include all others, as well. Do not differentiate between the value of one person over the value of any other.

Become a champion for the underprivileged populations. Lead with your heart to uplift the well-being of others with thankfulness that you are in a position to assist them. Invite others to pitch in and assist as they can. Step forward with resolve to create a fair and equitable world for all to enjoy.

Every time a person champions the well-being of those undergoing difficulties they cannot manage alone, that person sets an example for the rest of humanity to follow. One person can inspire many people to open their hearts and minds to the plight of those with overwhelming life challenges. Often, all it takes to inspire other people to extend themselves to benefit people in need is to share a person's accounts of when they received help.

As people extend themselves with openhearted goodness, the best in humanity shines forth. Humanity consists of brothers and sisters within the family of mankind. Unfortunately, this family could be taking much better care of their family members.

If everyone felt like they were a beloved member of a very special family, all would be respectful to everyone else in that family. Each would treasure one another and contribute to the rest of the family's well-being. Humanity is missing the big picture when they do not perceive all people as sisters and brothers.

Model yourself after those who exhibit high principles of inclusion and treasuring of all people. Keep going in the right direction, considering all people as sisters and brothers within the same family. Rejoice that your relatives are all over the world, in every country on Earth.

Be pleased that your family is varied, with many having different characteristics, skills, and talents. Feel grateful for the variety within your family. Recognize each person's specialness and be thankful for your own uniqueness.

If everyone on Earth shared these views, our planet would be a more pleasant place to live. People would be more inclined to honor and respect all others, becoming more receptive to other people's perspectives. Then all people's viewpoints would most likely become more expansive.

Continuing on the path that we have been on puts brakes on our evolutionary progress when we have no time to waste. We have already wasted too much time. We have listened to and ignored experts who advocate restricting wastefulness to preserve Earth's well-being. Teenagers, it is up to you to protect our planetary home.

Time goes by, yet the same problems remain. Populations neglect to do all they can to avoid increasing pollution. Instead, people prefer to wait and wait and wait until they become convinced that they have no other alternative.

Without a firm commitment to conserving natural resources, humanity will continue to drain Earth's natural resources without limit. Humanity does not think ahead and make rational decisions. Like spoiled children, Earth's inhabitants do not choose to behave sensibly.

Only quick, decisive action to forestall continued negligence on the part of humanity will keep our planetary home secure. There needs to be a reversal in certain attitudes and behaviors within society at large. Create impetus to erect restrictions to keep people from stripping Earth of her ability to continue serving humanity's needs. People need to safeguard Earth's viability for future generations.

Lead with your determination to honor and respect all people and their rights as human beings.

Place loving arms around all people. Especially include people of differing races. Never discount the importance of any person. Hold every person as precious and respect all, always.

CHAPTER FIFTEEN

VALUE EVERY PERSON

Are you familiar with the word *duty*? The word *duty* gives the impression that you must do something that you do not want to do. However, there is another aspect to the word *duty*. It conveys the right and honorable course of action. Every person's duty is to contribute to the well-being of other people. Even small kindnesses produce uplifting feelings for both those on the giving end and those on the receiving end.

Be alert to ways you can help another person. When you see someone who needs support, stand by their side. Sometimes that is all that one can do. However, this small act of caring can significantly bolster the other person's fortitude. There are endless ways to show people that you care about them.

Do not take your cues from the world around you. Your world is awash with uncaring attitudes and disregard for the preciousness of all people. Those attitudes bring destruction, heartache, and pain. They also promote moral decay within those who discount the importance of every person.

If you tend to believe that certain people are innately inferior, get rid of that discriminatory mindset. Only insecure people maneuver to elevate themselves as being superior to others. Keep yourself and everyone else on a level playing field. Do not have different standards of behavior depending on the person with whom you are interacting. When you give respect, you deserve the respect that then flows back to you.

Value yourself and every other person. Everyone has challenges, and for some, their challenges are overwhelming. Whatever you do, do not add to another person's burdens. If you cannot interact with respect and civility, do not interact at all.

When teenagers bring out the best in their selves, they build self-esteem. Many teenagers feel wobbly and that they do not fit in as well as the rest of the students do. Introverted teenagers, in particular, may be hesitant to sign up for extracurricular activities. However, those who forge ahead to participate in those activities that appeal to them set themselves up for success.

Teenagers are a lot like Columbus. Columbus was on a journey of discovery. He was looking for a new world. Teenagers are on their own journey of discovery. They are stepping out of childhood and taking on the challenges of becoming a responsible adult.

Teenagers, who naturally have within them the will to do good, will create life satisfaction for themselves. Those who regard every other person admirably ultimately feel more self-assured. They know they are taking the right and honorable path in life, which builds self-confidence.

If every person was fair-minded and kind-hearted, our world would be pleasant for everyone. People would behave nobly, being eager to help others while thoroughly enjoying the opportunity to be of assistance. As a result, everyone's self-esteem would flourish.

Self-esteem is like fresh air and sunshine. It makes a person feel good inside. When a person has a positive perception of themself, they are more willing to reach out to others.

When people care about the well-being of other people, they are more inclined to step forward to support them and offer assistance that person could not generate for themself. Not until one is in the position of requiring assistance beyond their capability to obtain can one truly appreciate the relief experienced by the person being aided. People helping other people reflect the better side of humanity.

Every person can choose the high road in life. When a person chooses the high road, they make a commitment to respect all other people. This commitment becomes the cornerstone of their life. Respecting all others is a big step for many people, a step that everyone needs to take.

Becoming a respectful person is the first of several steps one must take to fulfill their potential to be a positive force for good in the world. Teenagers do not realize that they have the capacity to change the way people, in general, interact with one another. By setting respectful standards of interaction with all other people, teenagers take on the role of educating their contemporaries and also their elders.

Everyone experiences an expansion of self-worth when they express their inner goodness. The most caring people consistently feel love for all while going about their daily lives. Many contribute to the well-being of humanity by working with charitable causes. These are divine worker bees who hum with charitable activity.

Every person has the capacity to serve the well-being of other people. Can you imagine a world where people care about other people to the extent of offering assistance broadly whenever the need arises? Can you imagine a world of kindness and compassion where every person cares about the well-being of every man, woman, and child?

Our human race has an unstated objective, the reason why we are alive. Simply put, each person is living on Earth to learn to accept all other people as sisters and brothers within a very large and gifted family. Unfortunately, this large family has a problem. The family fails to recognize their own family members.

Certain family members are discounted as being of lesser importance than others are. Then those family members receive less respect and less support. Invalid suppositions trigger critical attitudes, which stick like glue and pass down from generation to generation. The family of man is losing its proper bearings and turning against itself.

Humanity has within it positivity and negativity. Expansion of inclusiveness is evident but to a limited extent. Frequently, those who overly value themselves have tended to discount those they look down on and may discriminate against. Those with power and arrogance hold sway. Then those without advanced education or financial assets may not garner as much respect, although they may be extraordinary contributors to the welfare of other people.

Our world is out of kilter as the rich get richer and the poor stay poor. Envision a world where all people go out of their way to uplift one another. Compassionate people can step forward to help the unemployed find job opportunities.

With an income, a family can relax and enjoy being together without the stress of potential eviction from their residence or of not being able to feed their family. **If you have the inclination to look down on another person, stop. Instead, think twice, get creative, and figure out how you can help them.**

Everyone has positive and negative attributes. Instead of obsessing over another person's wrongdoing, go within yourself and identify your own shortcomings. You cannot correct another person's poor behavior, but you can do away with your own lesser qualities. Clean your own house and leave it to other people to clean their own houses.

Appreciate other people's good qualities and your good qualities, as well. Do not wish you had another person's attributes. Identify and be grateful for your own positive characteristics. Do not think that you are of lesser importance than other people.

Truly honorable people consider all others as their sisters and brothers. They champion the well-being of other people, being willing to stand by the side of another person who needs support they are capable of providing. **They are color blind, kind-hearted, and fair-minded.**

If all people grew up in households that held these high standards, there would be loving acceptance of minorities and those who were of other nationalities and skin color. All people would feel that they are as important as all others. With self-esteem, people flourish.

Many people wish our world were a more compatible and friendly place to be. There is only one way to create a better world for all of us to enjoy. When we take the initiative to interact with others without regarding our differences as dividers, we expand our perception of all belonging to one family. What better way is there to encourage respect and caring for all people than to consider every other person as our sister or brother?

The more open-minded people among us already demonstrate their valuing of all nationalities of people. Congenial, openhearted people create joy and satisfaction for themselves when they welcome others into their circle of friends. Everyone enjoys meeting new people and having the opportunity to express their unique self.

When people shy away from getting to know people from different backgrounds, they close a door that may have brought them enjoyment had they left it open. Being a person who welcomes others into their life will increase one's enjoyment of other people. Those who are reluctant to reach out to newcomers may feel left out later on when the newcomers form good friendships with those who were initially more accepting of them. Good-hearted people who include newcomers into their circle of friends are rarely disappointed.

Every good deed extended to another person enriches a person's self-worth. Feelings of self-worth expand when people bring out the best in themselves. Expressions of personal kindness and generosity indicate that one's inner goodness is flowing forward.

A person knows when they are expressing their inner goodness. Their actions are devoid of any trace of hurtfulness. Their benign nature encourages others to be as they are. Self-respect comes easily to these gracious people. Everyone enjoys being with them, and they enjoy being with all others.

Everyone searches for satisfaction in life. Generally, people assume that their life will be fulfilling if they have ample financial assets. However, when people reach old age and look back over their life, excessive amounts of financial assets do not matter as they thought they would. By that time, most people take pleasure in the contributions they made during their lifetime. Their greatest satisfaction comes from remembering the ways they helped people.

When the end of one's life is near, typically, people assess how worthwhile their life has been. A common realization is that they are proud of some of the things they did, but they wish they had the benefit of knowing, while they were young, what they know to be true in old age. Older people would advise young people to take the high road in life so they would build their life satisfaction daily. **The high road consists of extending oneself to others with acts of kindness, promoting the well-being of others in ways large or small, never putting out one's foot to trip another person, and perceiving every other person as someone who is entitled to respect.**

Strive to make this an exemplary life for yourself, so you will be pleased that you passed the test of conducting yourself with honor. **Before your life ends, dig deep to uncover and express all the wonderful qualities, talents, and attributes you have. Do not compare yourself to any other person. Appreciate your individuality and enjoy being you!**

Truly honorable people consider all others as their sisters and brothers, and are color blind, kind-hearted, and fair-minded.

If you have the inclination to look down on another person, stop. Instead, think twice, get creative, and figure out how you can help them.

Each person is living on Earth to learn to accept all other people as sisters and brothers within a very large and gifted family.

DIVINE
RESOURCES
FOR ALL

The best way to live is to keep in mind what you are here to accomplish. Go beyond the typical aspirations. *God Talks to All of Us* enlightens you on how to live your best life. It's companion, *God Talks to All of Us, Thoughts to Keep in Mind*, is a pocket guide to help you stay on track with your efforts to evolve your life. *Teenagers, Be The Best You Can Be* guides teens and adults on a path to build the strength of their character. *What It Is Like to Die and What Comes After* will prepare you to move into the higher dimensions after your death, no matter the circumstances. To discover more about available resources on how to evolve, now and after death, visit DivineResourcesForAll.com.

God Talks to All of Us, With Love and Rationality, for Our Enlightenment is a powerful narrative direct from God clarifying why you are alive on Earth and empowering you to work towards the betterment of yourself and the protection of our planet.

Kay Mielenz developed an urgent desire to understand the significance of life. To her, it did not make sense if life had no purpose other than experiencing one's youth, middle age, old age, and then dying. One day, while meditating, she experienced a powerful presence blanketing her with extraordinarily high vibrations. Then she heard God speaking to her for the first time. His divine voice said, "I am Creator God, and I am going to dictate My communication to humanity for you to record and distribute. I want to speak to all of My children so they will understand My true nature."

God Talks to
All of Us,

Thoughts to
Keep in Mind

A Short Summary

Presented By
Kay Mielenz

This booklet contains selected excerpts from *God Talks to All of Us, With Love and Rationality, for Our Enlightenment* to support your daily endeavor to evolve your attitudes and behaviors. Keep in mind that even with a firm desire to advance your personal traits, your path will bring both successes and failures. Be patient with yourself and remain dedicated. Enjoy your feelings of well-being as they multiply.

You can find these books on Amazon, from DivineResourcesForAll.com and in all good bookstores.

What It Is Like to Die and What Comes After demonstrates what happens to people after they die. Deceased people tell their stories, which deliver insight into how to die with the assurance that one will easily transfer into a desirable afterlife. This book also contains messages to loved ones from those who are deceased. *What It Is Like to Die and What Comes After* is a must-read for anyone who wants to have documentation about what occurs when physical life ends.

Discover:
- Core insights that will prevent you from becoming stuck between this world and the next.
- Common pitfalls after dying and how to navigate them.
- Relief knowing there is a place for everyone within the heavens, even those who lived misguided lifetimes.
- Transformative knowledge that will allow you to face death without fear, by clearly understanding how to navigate what comes next.
- How to avoid after-life regrets.

www.ingramcontent.com/pod-product-compliance
Lightning Source LLC
Chambersburg PA
CBHW071015120626
46546CB00003B/1103